Contents

Index

Dallas, Texas	C5	74	Denver, Colorado	C6	74
Dover, Delaware	C11	75	Dublin, Ireland	E5	30

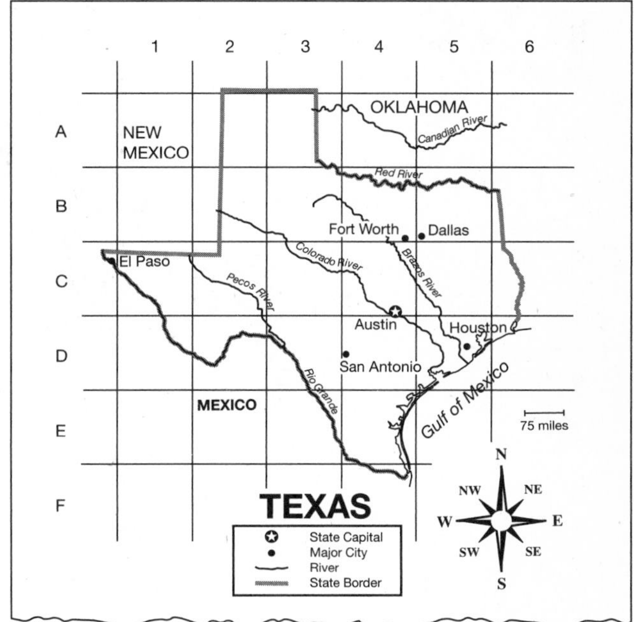

Features

Using Information Resources is designed as a supplement to your curriculum. Throughout school and in life, students need to be able to look up information in various resources and use text and visual features to gain information. This product will introduce students to resources and features, and it will build their confidence in using resources independently.

Each lesson is set up in a similar way.

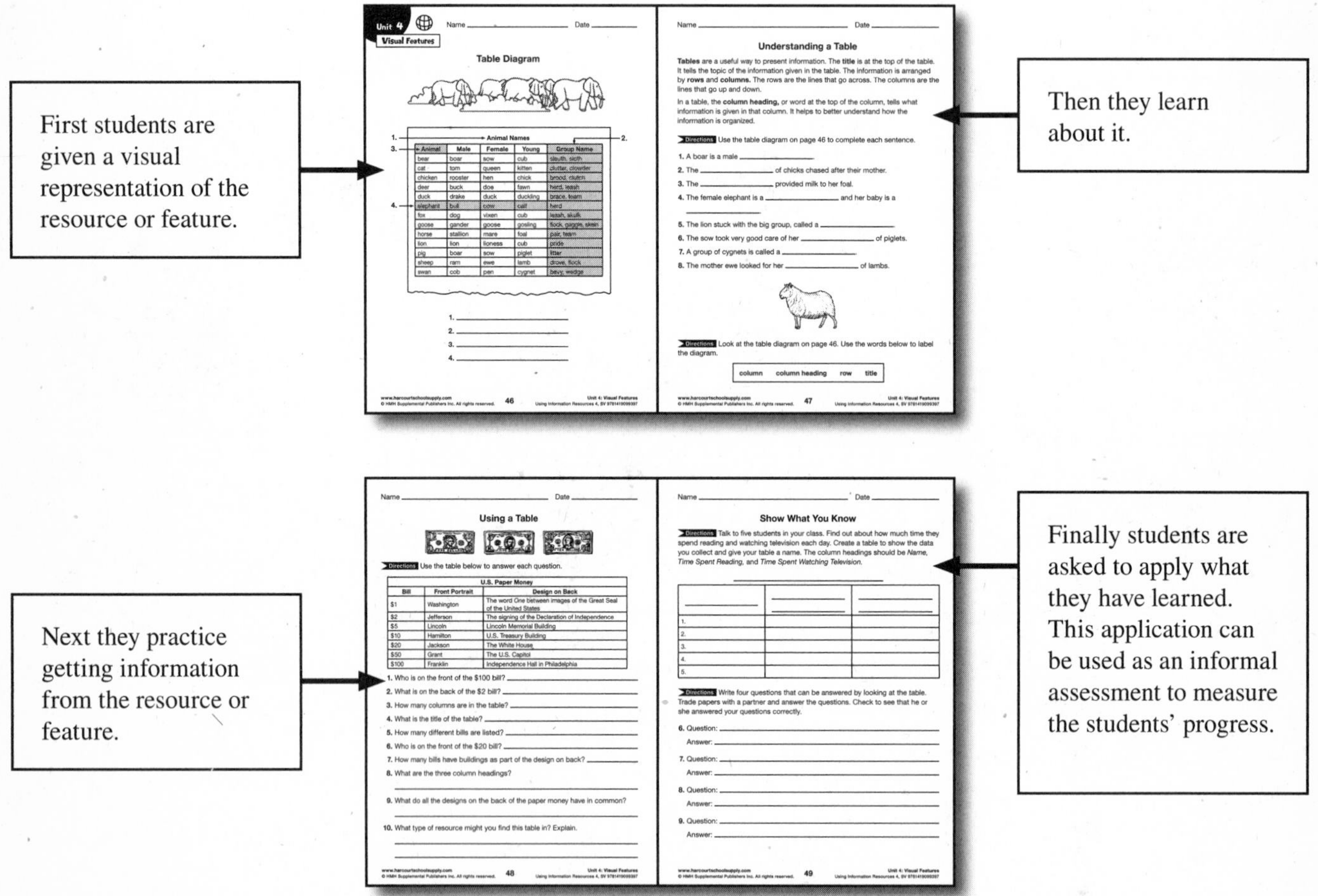

First students are given a visual representation of the resource or feature.
Then they learn about it.
Next they practice getting information from the resource or feature.
Finally students are asked to apply what they have learned. This application can be used as an informal assessment to measure the students' progress.

Unit 4 — Visual Features

Name ______ Date ______

Table Diagram

1. → Animal Names
2. ← (Group Name)
3. → (Animal)
4. → (elephant row)

Animal	Male	Female	Young	Group Name
bear	boar	sow	cub	sleuth, sloth
cat	tom	queen	kitten	clutter, clowder
chicken	rooster	hen	chick	brood, clutch
deer	buck	doe	fawn	herd, leash
duck	drake	duck	duckling	brace, team
elephant	bull	cow	calf	herd
fox	dog	vixen	cub	leash, skulk
goose	gander	goose	gosling	flock, gaggle, skein
horse	stallion	mare	foal	pair, team
lion	lion	lioness	cub	pride
pig	boar	sow	piglet	litter
sheep	ram	ewe	lamb	drove, flock
swan	cob	pen	cygnet	bevy, wedge

1. ______
2. ______
3. ______
4. ______

www.harcourtschoolsupply.com © HMH Supplemental Publishers Inc. All rights reserved. 46 Unit 4: Visual Features Using Information Resources 4, SV 9781419099397

Name ______ Date ______

Understanding a Table

Tables are a useful way to present information. The **title** is at the top of the table. It tells the topic of the information given in the table. The information is arranged by **rows** and **columns.** The rows are the lines that go across. The columns are the lines that go up and down.

In a table, the **column heading,** or word at the top of the column, tells what information is given in that column. It helps to better understand how the information is organized.

Directions Use the table diagram on page 46 to complete each sentence.

1. A boar is a male ______
2. The ______ of chicks chased after their mother.
3. The ______ provided milk to her foal.
4. The female elephant is a ______ and her baby is a ______
5. The lion stuck with the big group, called a ______
6. The sow took very good care of her ______ of piglets.
7. A group of cygnets is called a ______.
8. The mother ewe looked for her ______ of lambs.

Directions Look at the table diagram on page 46. Use the words below to label the diagram.

column column heading row title

www.harcourtschoolsupply.com © HMH Supplemental Publishers Inc. All rights reserved. 47 Unit 4: Visual Features Using Information Resources 4, SV 9781419099397

Name ______ Date ______

Using a Table

Directions Use the table below to answer each question.

U.S. Paper Money		
Bill	Front Portrait	Design on Back
$1	Washington	The word *One* between images of the Great Seal of the United States
$2	Jefferson	The signing of the Declaration of Independence
$5	Lincoln	Lincoln Memorial Building
$10	Hamilton	U.S. Treasury Building
$20	Jackson	The White House
$50	Grant	The U.S. Capitol
$100	Franklin	Independence Hall in Philadelphia

1. Who is on the front of the $100 bill? ______
2. What is on the back of the $2 bill? ______
3. How many columns are in the table? ______
4. What is the title of the table? ______
5. How many different bills are listed? ______
6. Who is on the front of the $20 bill? ______
7. How many bills have buildings as part of the design on back? ______
8. What are the three column headings? ______
9. What do all the designs on the back of the paper money have in common? ______
10. What type of resource might you find this table in? Explain. ______

www.harcourtschoolsupply.com © HMH Supplemental Publishers Inc. All rights reserved. 48 Unit 4: Visual Features Using Information Resources 4, SV 9781419099397

Name ______ Date ______

Show What You Know

Directions Talk to five students in your class. Find out about how much time they spend reading and watching television each day. Create a table to show the data you collect and give your table a name. The column headings should be *Name, Time Spent Reading,* and *Time Spent Watching Television.*

______	______	______
1.		
2.		
3.		
4.		
5.		

Directions Write four questions that can be answered by looking at the table. Trade papers with a partner and answer the questions. Check to see that he or she answered your questions correctly.

6. Question: ______
   Answer: ______
7. Question: ______
   Answer: ______
8. Question: ______
   Answer: ______
9. Question: ______
   Answer: ______

www.harcourtschoolsupply.com © HMH Supplemental Publishers Inc. All rights reserved. 49 Unit 4: Visual Features Using Information Resources 4, SV 9781419099397

This step-by-step approach introduces students to resources and guides them in using each resource in a meaningful way so that they internalize how to use it and understand why it is helpful. The lessons in Unit 3 follow this same approach, but in a three-page format. The visual representation and information for learning are combined on one page.

Because a dictionary is so rich with information and so important to a student's learning, the unit on dictionaries is set like the other lessons in the product but includes additional practice. The unit begins with the visual representation and ends with application. The lessons in between provide specific practice with all of the skills needed to use a dictionary effectively.

We hope that students will have fun, be challenged, and enjoy using information resources to learn!

Name ____________________ Date ____________

Dictionary Entries Diagram

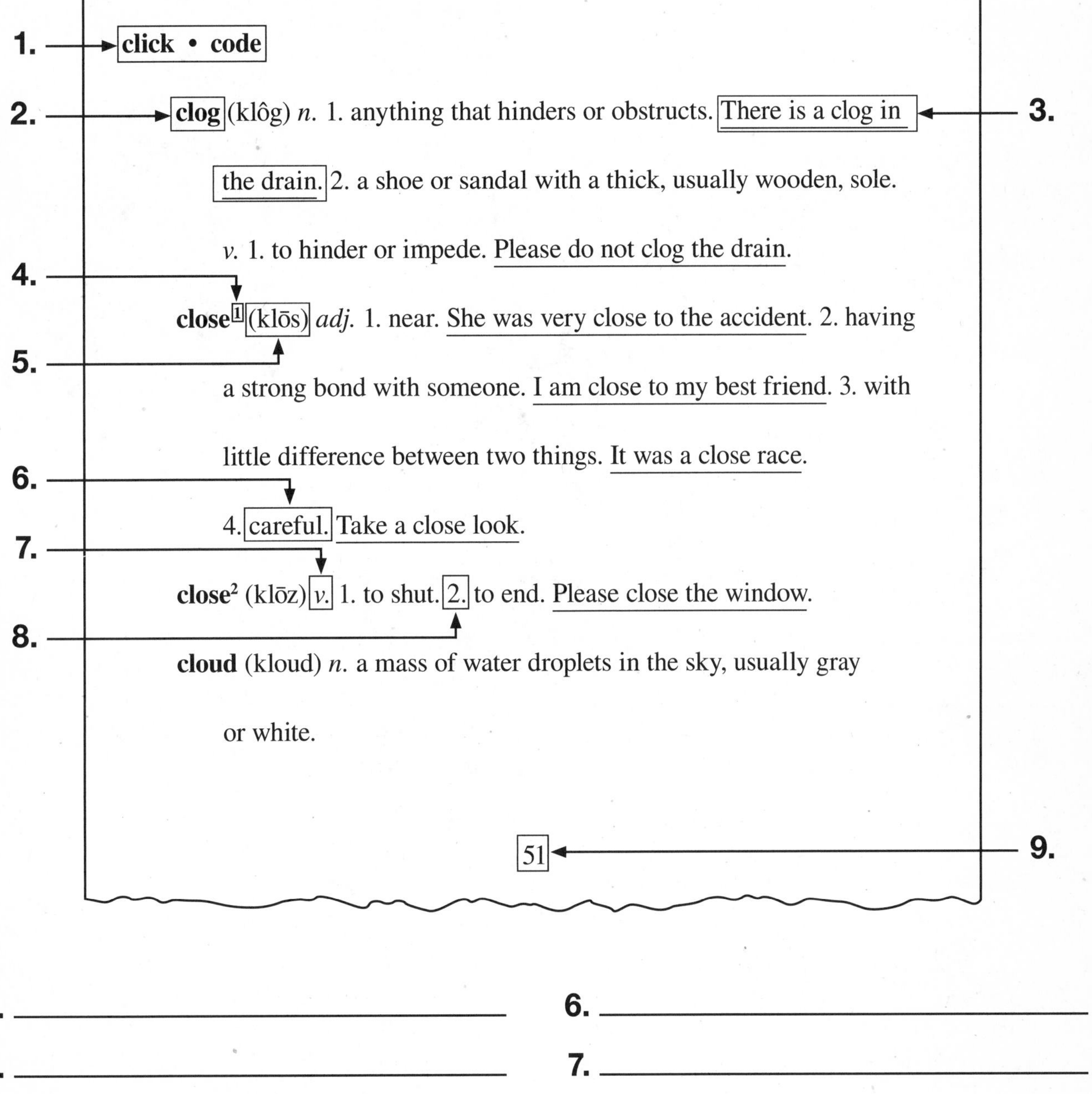

1. click • code
2. clog (klôg) n. 1. anything that hinders or obstructs. There is a clog in the drain. 2. a shoe or sandal with a thick, usually wooden, sole. v. 1. to hinder or impede. Please do not clog the drain. 3.
4.
close[1] (klōs) adj. 1. near. She was very close to the accident. 2. having a strong bond with someone. I am close to my best friend. 3. with little difference between two things. It was a close race.
5.
6.
4. careful. Take a close look.
7.
close[2] (klōz) v. 1. to shut. 2. to end. Please close the window.
8.
cloud (kloud) n. a mass of water droplets in the sky, usually gray or white.
51
9.

1. ____________________
2. ____________________
3. ____________________
4. ____________________
5. ____________________
6. ____________________
7. ____________________
8. ____________________
9. ____________________

Name ______________________ Date ______________

Learning About Dictionary Entries

Dictionaries are helpful in many ways. Each entry has special features to help better understand words.

The two words at the top of the page are called **guide words.** Guide words tell the first and last words on that page of the dictionary.

An **entry word** is a word that is defined in the dictionary. These are the words that are in alphabetical order on each page. Each entry word is in dark print.

The **pronunciation guide** spells the word in a way that helps sound it out. The spelling is in parentheses.

Just after the entry word or the pronunciation guide, the **part of speech** is listed.

- An *n.* means the word is a noun.
- A *v.* means the word is a verb.
- An *adj.* means the word is an adjective.
- An *adv.* means the word is an adverb.
- A *prep.* means the word is a preposition.

Entry words that are spelled the same way but have different meanings have **small raised numbers** at the end of each word. Here is an example.

- **alley**^{1} (al′ ē) *n.* a lane in a garden or park, bordered by trees or shrubs. <u>She walked in the alley.</u>
- **alley**^{2} (al′ ē) *n.* a fine marble used as the shooter in playing marbles. <u>He used the alley to knock the last marble out of the ring.</u>

The **definition** tells what the entry word means. If there is more than one definition, each is labeled with a **definition number.**

A **sample sentence** gives an example of how the entry word can be used. Each sample sentence is underlined.

A **page number** is placed on the bottom of each dictionary page.

Directions Look at the dictionary entries diagram on page 3. Use the words and definitions below to label each part.

definition	**definition number**	**entry word**
guide words	**page number**	**part of speech**
pronunciation guide	**raised number**	**sample sentence**

Name ______________________________ Date ______________

Reviewing Nouns

A **noun (n.)** is a word that names a person, place, or thing.

A **common noun** names any person, place, or thing. It is a general word that begins with a lowercase letter unless it is the first word in a sentence.

birthday girl parka

A **proper noun** names a specific person, place, or thing. A proper noun always begins with a capital letter. A dictionary will show which nouns are proper nouns.

Antarctica Mount McKinley Rover

Directions Read each sentence. Underline each common noun once. Underline each proper noun twice.

1. Eskimos live in the coldest places in the world.
2. Many of them live in Alaska, the largest state in the United States.
3. Other communities are found in Greenland and Canada.
4. These people have adjusted to very bitter temperatures.
5. Eskimos who live in the Arctic hunt polar bears.
6. The hunters also track walruses.
7. These animals are valuable for their meat and for their ivory tusks.
8. This hard material is used to make knives, hooks, and other tools.
9. For centuries Eskimos have used ice from the sea for their fresh drinking water.
10. They speak a language that is different from the speech of other Native Americans.
11. Many Eskimos once lived in special homes.
12. These buildings were called igloos.

Name ______________________ Date ____________

Reviewing Pronouns

A **pronoun (pron.)** is a word that takes the place of one or more nouns.

My father and I like to watch *birds.* *We* like to watch *them.*

Some common pronouns are *I, we, he, she, it, they, them, us, him, her,* and *me.*

Directions Read each sentence. Think of a pronoun to take the place of the underlined words. Write the pronoun on the line.

1. My father went to the store to get a bird book. ____________
2. My father and I put a bird feeder in the yard. ____________
3. We began to watch the birds when they came to the feeder. ____________
4. Birds are the only creatures that have feathers. ____________
5. Birds have bodies that help the birds to fly. ____________
6. The many types of birds fascinated my father and me. ____________
7. The bird book helped us to name some of the birds. ____________
8. We looked in the bird book to find facts. ____________
9. Soon my father and I will watch the young birds fly. ____________

Directions On the lines below, write five sentences without pronouns describing your favorite thing to do with your family. Trade papers with a partner. On another sheet of paper, rewrite each other's sentences, replacing pronouns with nouns wherever possible.

10. ____

Name ____________________ Date ____________

Reviewing Adjectives

An **adjective (adj.)** is a word that describes a noun or pronoun.

That monkey looks *happy.*

An adjective can tell how many.

Some animals have been injured.

Directions Read each sentence. Together the sentences tell a short story, but they are not in the right order. Complete each sentence with an adjective from the box. Then renumber the sentences in the correct order to tell the story. Write the story on the lines below.

good	**grateful**	**injured**	**kind**	**poor**	**soft**	**strong**

_____ **1.** The girl put a bandage on the ____________ leg.

_____ **2.** The animal and the girl remained ____________ friends.

_____ **3.** A ____________ girl rescued the animal.

_____ **4.** A ____________ animal was caught in a trap.

_____ **5.** Then she gave the animal a ____________ bed.

_____ **6.** Soon the ____________ animal was ____________ enough to take care of itself.

7. ____

____

____

____

____

____

____

____

Name ______________________ Date ____________

Reviewing Verbs

An **action verb (v.)** is a word that describes action.

People *drive* across the county.

A **linking verb (v.)** describes a state of being. It connects an adjective or a noun to the subject.

I *am* calm. Sandra *looks* lovely.

Directions Read each sentence. Choose the action or linking verb from the box to complete each sentence. Use each verb once.

appeared	**ate**	**flew**	**lives**
looked	**moved**	**roared**	**seems**
slept	**tasted**	**was**	**were**

1. My family ______________ in California.
2. My aunt ______________ to Pennsylvania two years ago.
3. Pennsylvania ______________ so far away.
4. We ______________ on a huge jet to go visit her.
5. When the jet was in the sky, the houses below ______________ so small.

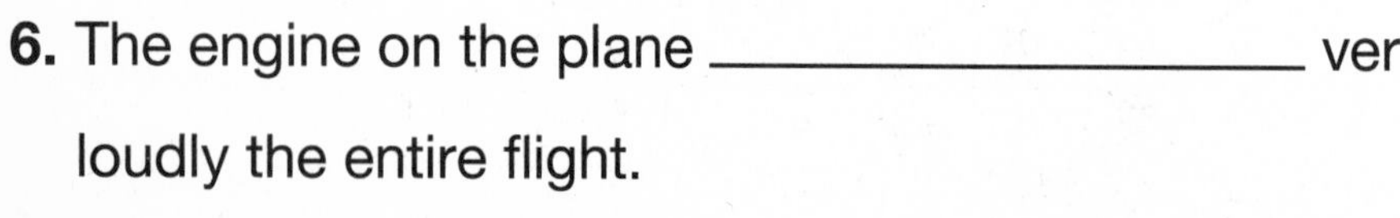

6. The engine on the plane ______________ very loudly the entire flight.
7. My aunt ______________ for us.
8. She ______________ excited to see us.
9. We ______________ all very happy.
10. Later in the day, we ______________ at a new restaurant.
11. The food ______________ delicious.
12. We ______________ soundly after a busy day!

Name ______________________________ Date ______________

Reviewing Adverbs

An **adverb (adv.)** is a word that tells more about a verb.

Some adverbs tell how an action takes place. Most of these kinds of adverbs end in the letters *-ly.*

The train pulled *quickly* out of the station.

Some adverbs tell when an action takes place.

The train left *yesterday.*

Some adverbs tell where an action takes place.

We were *here* when it left.

Directions Complete the sentences by adding words from the box that tell how, when, or where. Use each word once.

busily	**carefully**	**excitedly**	**finally**	**happily**	**Here**
quickly	**quietly**	**slowly**	**tomorrow**	**upstairs**	**wearily**

1. The children called ____________ to each other. (how)
2. They knew that ____________ they would be going to pick apples. (when)
3. They looked forward ____________ to when they would leave. (how)
4. When the time came, the children ____________ climbed into the car. (how)
5. Their mother drove ____________ to the orchard. (how)
6. "____________ we are!" she exclaimed. (where)
7. The children ____________ picked the biggest, brightest apples. (how)
8. The baskets seemed to be filling ____________. (how)
9. The baskets were ____________ filled. (when)
10. The children ____________ climbed back into the car. (how)
11. They talked ____________ about their day. (how)
12. They were very tired when they went ____________ to bed. (where)

Name ______________________ Date ______________

Reviewing Contractions

A **contraction (contr.)** is a shortened form of two words.

he + is = he's

An **apostrophe (')** takes the place of one or more letters in a contraction.

are + not = aren't

have + not = haven't

has + not = hasn't

can + not = can't

do + not = don't

was + not = wasn't

were + not = weren't

had + not = hadn't

did + not = didn't

should + not = shouldn't

would + not = wouldn't

Directions Underline the contraction in each sentence. Write the words that make each contraction on the line.

1. Tonya doesn't like to play softball at school. ______________
2. She isn't fond of sports. ______________
3. Tonya hasn't been getting enough exercise. ______________
4. She thinks she isn't good at sports. ______________
5. Tonya cannot be healthy if she doesn't exercise. ______________
6. Tonya wouldn't even try to play softball. ______________
7. Tonya's coaches weren't happy. ______________
8. Tonya's parents don't know what to do. ______________
9. Tonya's parents haven't noticed that Tonya likes tennis. ______________
10. Tonya's parents shouldn't make her play softball. ______________

Name ______________________ Date ____________

Reviewing Prefixes

A **prefix** is a group of letters added to the beginning of a word to change its meaning.

Sue is happy. Sue is unhappy.

Prefix	Meaning	Example
dis	not	dislike
im	not	impossible
in	not	inactive
mis	incorrectly	misspell
non	not	nonstop
pre	before	prepay
re	again	reread
re	back	return
un	not	unfair
un	opposite of	undo

Directions Read each sentence. Add a prefix to each underlined word to create the meaning of the word in parentheses. Write each word on the line. Use the list above to help you.

1. Tony was fair to keep Tara's doll. (not) ____________
2. He should have turned it to her. (back) ____________
3. Tara is able to understand why he took the doll. (not) ____________
4. She understood what he wanted to do. (incorrectly) ____________
5. Tony had planned how he would take the doll. (before) ____________
6. He waited patiently to see what Tara would do. (not) ____________
7. He wanted to pay her for losing his baseball card. (again) ____________
8. When Tony saw how happy Tara was, he felt sorry. (not) ____________
9. He was pleased with the way things had gone. (not) ____________
10. Tony turned the doll and apologized to Tara. (back) ____________

Name ______________________ Date ____________

Reviewing Suffixes

A **suffix** is added to the end of a root word to change its meaning.

help   helpless

Suffix	Meaning	Example
al	like, referring to	coastal
able, ible	able to be	breakable, flexible
er, or	one who	singer, sailor
ful	full of	helpful
less	without	hopeless
y	what kind	snowy
ly	how	quickly
ist	one who does	artist

Directions Read each sentence. Circle the words with a suffix. Then write what the suffix means on the line.

1. It was a dark, stormy night. ______________
2. A visitor came to my door. ______________
3. He politely asked if he could come in from the rain. ______________
4. The man's musical voice charmed me. ______________
5. He sat by my fire and told wonderful stories. ______________
6. The stories were full of magical characters. ______________
7. He told me about unforgettable travels and adventures. ______________
8. I told the man his stories were amazing but unbelievable. ______________
9. These things all really happened to the storyteller! ______________

Name ______________________ Date ______________

Using a Pronunciation Guide

An important part of most dictionaries is the **pronunciation guide.** This helps the reader know how to say new words. Each word has a pronunciation next to it with symbols that show how to sound it out. This is called a **phonetic spelling.** The guide explains what the symbols mean. It also gives a familiar word in which the sound is heard.

The words in the dictionary are also divided into **syllables.** Syllables are parts of words that have only one vowel sound. The syllable that is pronounced most strongly will have an accent mark (′). This also helps the reader to say the word correctly. In some dictionaries, the strongest syllable will be written in dark print. For example, the word *habit* may look like one of the following.

hab′ it   **hab** it

Directions Read each pronunciation. Using the pronunciation guide, circle the word that matches the pronunciation. Write how many syllables are in the word on the line.

a	add	**i**	it	**o͝o**	took	**oi**	oil
ā	ace	**ī**	ice	**o͞o**	pool	**ou**	pout
â	care	**o**	odd	**u**	up	**ng**	ring
ä	palm	**ō**	open	**û**	burn	**th**	thin
e	end	**ô**	order	**yo͞o**	fuse	**t͟h**	this
ē	equal					**zh**	vision

ə = { a in *above*   e in *sicken*   i in *possible*   o in *melon*   u in *circus* }

HBJ School Dictionary

1. pär′ kə	party	parka	______
2. snō	snow	sun	______
3. mə shēn′	matching	machine	______
4. kar′ ə bo͞o	caribou	carbon	______
5. fä′ thər	feather	father	______
6. sur prīz′	surplus	surprise	______
7. līt	light	let	______
8. di zīn′	dizzy	design	______

Name ______________________________ Date ______________

Words with Multiple Meanings

Words that have the same spelling but different meanings are called **homographs.** Homographs are listed in the dictionary as separate entry words with numbers. Look at the example.

felt[1] *n.* a soft kind of cloth. He used felt in his art project.

felt[2] *v.* sensed something through touch. She felt the soft fur.

Some homographs are pronounced differently.

wind[1] *n.* moving air. The wind blew violently during the storm.

wind[2] *v.* to turn a knob on something, such as a clock. He needs to wind the clock each day.

Directions Write a new sentence using a homograph for the underlined word. Use a dictionary if you need help.

1. Manny will lead Tony to the tide pool to show him the crabs.

____

2. Manny has a small wound on his toe from a crab bite.

____

3. Tony was last to be pinched.

____

4. There is a tear in Tony's sock!

____

5. Manny and Tony should not get too close to crabs.

____

Directions On another sheet of paper, make a list of all of the homographs you can think of. Compare your list with your classmates' lists. What is the greatest number of meanings for one homograph on the list?

Name ______________________________ Date ______________

Using Guide Words and Entry Words

The words in a dictionary are listed in alphabetical order. Each page of a dictionary has **guide words** at the top. They are the first and last words on the page. The word on the left is the first word on the page, and the word on the right is the last word on the page. Look at the example.

million • modern

The words *minute* and *model* will appear on this page.
The words *man* and *music* will not.

Entry words are the words that are defined in the dictionary. Every entry word on a page will fall in alphabetical order between each set of guide words.

Directions Circle each entry word that would be on a page with each set of guide words.

1. alive • arrest	2. flame • fourth	3. settle • sink
anxious	fourth	side
amount	flower	shawl
accept	fog	seed
arrest	figure	seventeen
actor	fly	sink
alive	flame	service
also	fox	settle
adventure	flew	sign
ant	from	sleep
ashes	flight	shelter

Directions Rewrite each group of words in alphabetical order. Then write the words that would be the guide words for each group.

4. ____________ • ____________

lawn ____________
last ____________
lamp ____________
late ____________

5. ____________ • ____________

palm ____________
page ____________
pass ____________
pad ____________

Name ______________________ Date ____________

Using a Dictionary

Directions Use the sample dictionary page below to answer each question.

member • mine

mere[1] (mēr) *adj.* 1. nothing more or other than; only. A mere girl moved the big stone. 2. unmixed; pure.

mere[2] (mēr) *n.* 1. a lake or pond. 2. a marsh.

mere[3] (mēr) *n.* a boundary.

meteor (mēt′ ē ər, mēt′ ē ôr) *n.* a piece of rock or metal from space that enters Earth's atmosphere at high speed, burns, and forms a streak of light as it falls to Earth.

microscopic (mī′ krə skäp′ ik) *adj.* so small as to be invisible or obscure except through a microscope. The DNA is microscopic.

migrate (mī′ grāt) *v.* 1. to move from one country or region to another. 2. to move from one region to another with the change in seasons, as many birds and some fish do. **migration** *n.*

mind (mīnd) *n.* 1. memory; recollection or remembrance. 2. what one thinks; opinion. He spoke his mind.
v. 1. to attend to. Please mind the baby. 2. to be careful of. 3. to object to.

1. What are the guide words on this page? ____________

2. How many entry words are shown in this sample? ____________

3. What part of speech is *mind* when it means "to attend to"? ____________

4. Which word is a homograph? ____________

5. How many different pronunciations does the homograph have? ____________

6. What noun has *migrate* as a root word and means "a group migrating together"? ____________

7. What verb has the same vowel sound as the letter *a* in *face?* ____________

8. Could the word *minute* be on this page? ____________

9. Which word has two different pronunciations? ____________

10. Choose one entry word from this page. Write a sentence that uses the word.

____

Name ______________________ Date ____________

Show What You Know

Directions When you find the meanings of words in a dictionary, you are adding new words to your vocabulary. Find the meanings for the words in the list and write them on the lines. Then write a clue in the space below the definition to help you remember each meaning. The clue could be a drawing, a synonym, an antonym, an example, or a non-example. The first one is done for you.

1. artistic _of art or artists_

____

clue: paintbrush

2. collage ______________________________

____

clue:

3. creative ______________________________

____

clue:

4. perspective ______________________________

____

clue:

5. sculpture ______________________________

____

clue:

Directions Write a paragraph about art on a separate sheet of paper. Use at least four of your new words.

Name ____________________ Date ____________

Online Catalog Diagram

Online Catalog Search

Catalog			
Find	**Options**	**Start Over**	**Help**
Author	Charles Arnold		
Title			
Subject			
Press Enter to select the highlighted command.			

Search Results

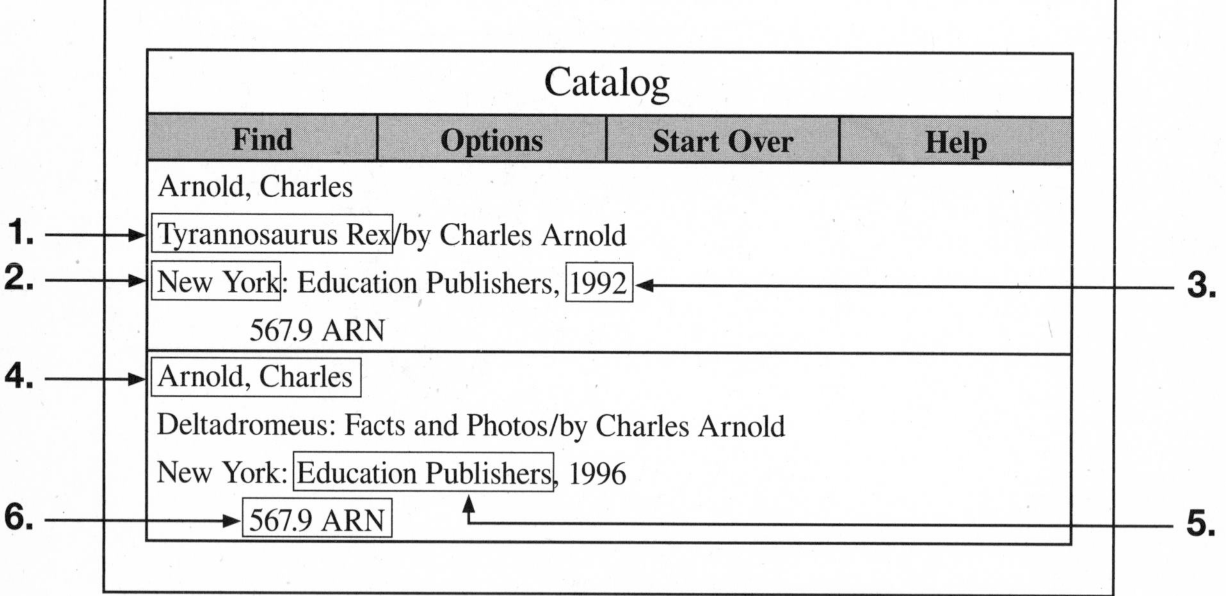

Catalog			
Find	**Options**	**Start Over**	**Help**

Arnold, Charles

1. → Tyrannosaurus Rex/by Charles Arnold

2. → New York: Education Publishers, 1992 ← 3.

567.9 ARN

4. → Arnold, Charles

Deltadromeus: Facts and Photos/by Charles Arnold

New York: Education Publishers, 1996

6. → 567.9 ARN ← 5. (Education Publishers)

1. ____________________ 4. ____________________

2. ____________________ 5. ____________________

3. ____________________ 6. ____________________

AUTHOR ? Call number (Dewey number)?
Publishing Co.? Title? City published in?
Year of publication?

Name ____________________ Date ____________________

Understanding an Online Catalog

In a library, an **online catalog** or a traditional card catalog is used to find any book or periodical (magazine) the library owns. The three main ways to search for a book in a library's catalog are by *author, title,* or *subject.* The computer will search its database of books and periodicals to find matches for the keyword that was entered.

When an author search is made, a list of all the books the author has written will be created. When a title search is made, a list of books whose titles contain the keyword will be created. When a subject search is made, a list of all the books related to that subject will be created. By clicking on a book from the list, more information will appear on that particular book.

Libraries arrange books in two main categories: fiction and nonfiction. Books that contain stories made up by the author are called fiction books. They are arranged in alphabetical order by the author's last name.

Nonfiction books contain factual information and are grouped by subject. Each subject has its own range of numbers called **call numbers.** The call numbers tell where the book is located on the shelves. Each book has a call number printed on its spine.

When a book title search is conducted, an information screen will appear if the library owns the book. The information screen provides the book's title and author. If the book is nonfiction, it will also show the book's call number.

When using an online catalog, it is important to understand the terms related to the book. The **author** is the person who wrote the book; the **title** is the name of the book; the call number tells information about a nonfiction book; the **city of publication** names the city where the book was published; the **publishing company** tells which company put the book together; and the **year published** tells the year the book became available to the public.

Directions Use the words below to help you label the online catalog search results on page 18.

author	**call number**	**city of publication**
publishing company	**title**	**year published**

Name ______________________ Date ______________

Using an Online Catalog

Directions Use the online catalog search and search results on page 18 to answer each question.

1. What are the titles of the books listed in the catalog? ______________________

____

2. Who is the publisher of the books? ______________________

3. How can you get more information on the book *Deltadromeus: Facts and Photos?* ______________________

Directions Use the catalog to answer each question.

Online Catalog Search

Catalog			
Find	**Options**	**Start Over**	**Help**

Author: Eoin Colfer

Title: Artemis Fowl: The Opal Deception

Published: New York: Hyperion Books for Children, 2005

Subjects: Fairies, Magic, Adventure

Notes: Artemis Fowl, having reverted to his criminal lifestyle following his last run-in with the fairies, travels to Berlin intending to steal a famous painting from a German bank, not realizing that his old rival, Opal Koboi, has been waiting for a chance to destroy him.

4. What is the best type of keyword search to get to this information page?

____

____

5. What other subjects can you search that might list this title as a result?

____

____

Name ______________________________ Date ______________

Show What You Know

Directions Use your library's online catalog to search the subject *mummies.* Select one book from the search results to answer each question.

1. What is the name of the book? ______________________________
2. Who is the author of the book? ______________________________
3. Who published the book? ______________________________
4. When was the book published? ______________________________
5. Do you think the book will be grouped by subject or alphabetically by the author's last name? Why? ______________________________

   ____
6. How can you find more books written by this author? ______________________________

   ____
7. Look at the cover of the book you selected. Write three things you think you would learn about in this book in the left-hand column. Then look in the book to find information about each of these three topics. Write what you find in the right-hand column.

Topics I Think I Will Learn About	What I Learned About Each Topic

Name ____________________ Date ____________

Atlas Diagram

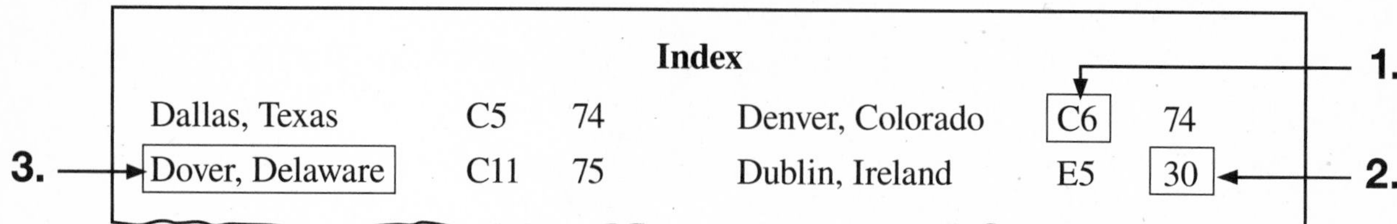

Index

Dallas, Texas	C5	74	Denver, Colorado	C6	74
Dover, Delaware	C11	75	Dublin, Ireland	E5	30

1.
2.
3.
4.

1 2 3 4 5 6

A B C D E F

NEW MEXICO

OKLAHOMA

Canadian River

Red River

Fort Worth

Dallas

El Paso

Colorado River

Brazos River

Pecos River

Austin

Houston

San Antonio

Rio Grande

MEXICO

Gulf of Mexico

75 miles

N NE E SE S SW W NW

TEXAS

State Capital
Major City
River
State Border

74

5.
6.
7.
8.
9.

1. ____________________ 6. ____________________

2. ____________________ 7. ____________________

3. ____________________ 8. ____________________

4. ____________________ 9. ____________________

5. ____________________

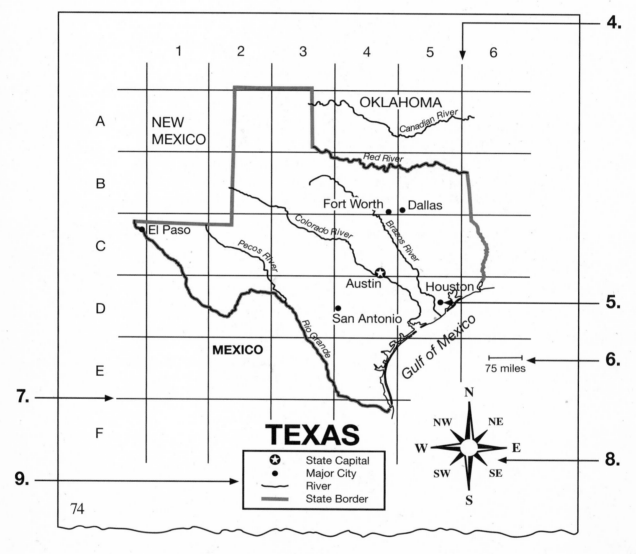

Name ______________________________ Date ______________

Understanding an Atlas

An **atlas** is a book of maps that shows the location of continents, countries, cities, landforms, and bodies of water. It also shows special features, such as the location of major airports. Learn to use this helpful resource.

- Use the map title.
  The **title** tells the subject of the map.
- Use a map scale.
  Most maps use the bar **scale** for finding distances. The scale compares real distance in miles or kilometers to the reduced map.
- Use lines of latitude and longitude.
  Lines of latitude go across the map, or east to west. **Lines of longitude** go up and down on a map, or north to south. These lines help to locate places.
- Use an index.
  Most atlases have an **index** to help find a place easily. The index provides the **coordinates** to help locate the **position point** of the **place.** For example, look at the index diagram on page 22 to locate the city for the coordinates B5. The place where the coordinates meet is the position point Dallas, Texas.
- Use map symbols and legends.
  A **symbol** is something that represents, or stands for, another thing. Features on a map such as cities, rivers, and lakes are represented with symbols. The **legend** tells what the symbols mean.
- Use a compass rose.
  The **compass rose** shows the directions north (N), south (S), east (E), and west (W) on a map.

Directions Use the words below to help you label the atlas diagram on page 22.

compass rose	**coordinates**	**legend**	**line of latitude**
line of longitude	**page number**	**place**	**position point**
scale	**title**		

Name ______________________________ Date ______________

Using an Atlas

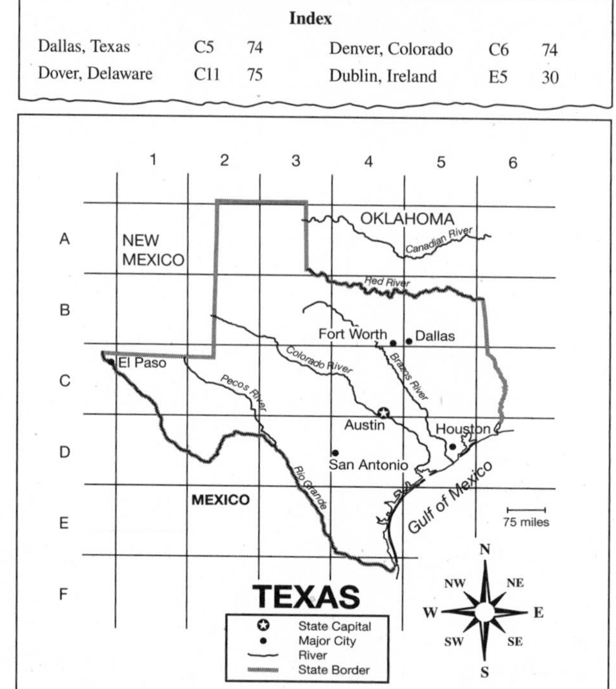

Index

Dallas, Texas	C5	74	Denver, Colorado	C6	74
Dover, Delaware	C11	75	Dublin, Ireland	E5	30

Directions Look at the atlas diagram above to answer each question.

1. On what page in the atlas would you find Dover, Delaware? ______________
2. At which coordinates in the atlas would you find Dublin, Ireland? ______________
3. On what page in the atlas would you find Denver, Colorado? ______________
4. In what direction is Austin located in relation to Dallas? ______________
5. Which river runs along the northeastern state border of Texas?

   ____
6. What is the state capital of Texas? ______________
7. What body of water is located at coordinates E-6? ______________
8. In what direction is El Paso located in relation to Austin? ______________
9. What major city is located at coordinates D-5? ______________
10. What river separates Texas from Mexico? ______________
11. What city is located at coordinates C-4? ______________
12. What coordinates does the Pecos River run through? ______________

Name ______________________ Date ____________

Show What You Know

Directions Use a world atlas from your classroom or school library to answer each question.

1. Use the index to find the country Spain. On what page or pages can it be found? ______________________

2. Use the index to find the city Portland, Oregon. What are the page and coordinates where it can be found? ______________________

3. Find Antarctica in the table of contents. On what page does the section on Antarctica start? ______________________

4. Turn to a map of Europe. What are the coordinates for London, England?

   ____

5. Turn to a map of South America. What is the largest country on this continent?

   ____

6. Turn to a map of Asia. What country is located south of Nepal? ______________________

7. Turn to the table of contents. How many different types of world maps are listed? ______________________

8. Turn to the map of the United States of America. What body of water is located at about 42°N latitude and 113°W longitude? ______________________

Directions Write two questions that can be answered by using your atlas. Trade with a partner. Check to see that your partner answered your questions correctly.

9. Question: ______________________

   Answer: ______________________

   Question: ______________________

   Answer: ______________________

Name ______________________ Date ____________

Thesaurus Diagram

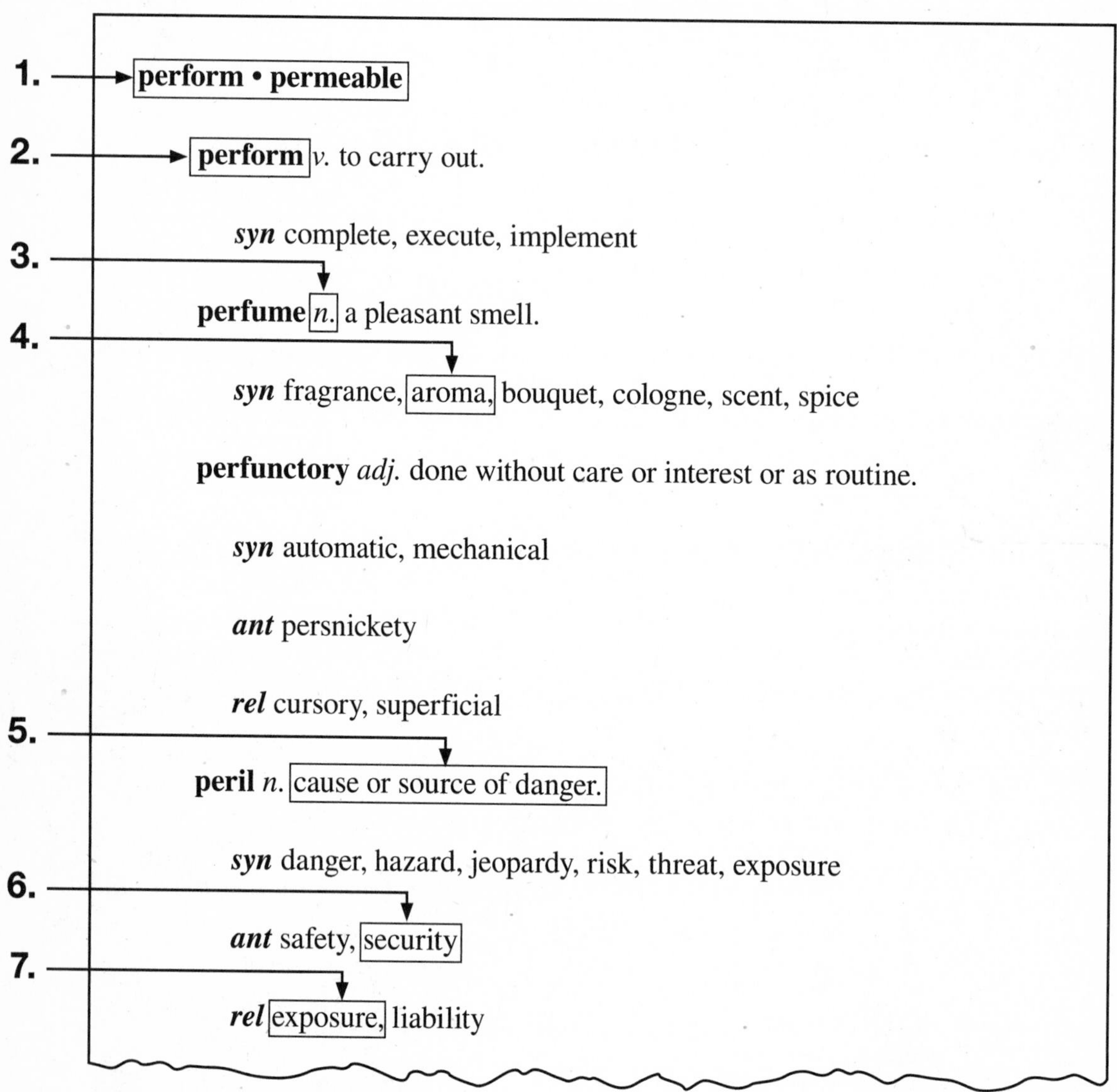

1.
perform • permeable
2.
perform v. to carry out.
syn complete, execute, implement
3.
perfume n. a pleasant smell.
4.
syn fragrance, aroma, bouquet, cologne, scent, spice
perfunctory adj. done without care or interest or as routine.
syn automatic, mechanical
ant persnickety
rel cursory, superficial
5.
peril n. cause or source of danger.
syn danger, hazard, jeopardy, risk, threat, exposure
6.
ant safety, security
7.
rel exposure, liability

1. ______________________
2. ______________________
3. ______________________
4. ______________________
5. ______________________
6. ______________________
7. ______________________

Name ______________________________ Date ______________

Understanding a Thesaurus

A **thesaurus** is a reference book that contains **synonyms** and **antonyms** for many words. Synonyms are words that have a similar or like meaning to each other. Antonyms are words that have the opposite meaning. A thesaurus helps the user find words that more exactly express what he or she is trying to say. A thesaurus can also be used to choose words that can improve writing by making it more interesting and lively.

- Like a dictionary, a thesaurus has **guide words** at the top of each page. The guide words tell the first and last words on that page.
- The **entry words** are presented alphabetically in dark print. Entry words are the words you look up to replace with a synonym or antonym.
- The **part of speech** follows each entry word.
- A brief **definition** is given after the part of speech.
- **Related words** are words that are almost, but not quite, synonyms for the entry word.

Directions Use the thesaurus diagram on page 26 to answer each question.

1. How many synonyms does *perfunctory* have? ______________________
2. What are the guide words for this sample page? ______________________
3. List one antonym for *peril.* ______________________
4. The entry words are listed in alphabetical order. Explain why this helpful.

____

____

5. Could the word *pesky* be found on this page in the thesaurus? ____________

Directions Use the words below to label the thesaurus diagram on page 26.

antonym	**definition**	**entry word**	**guide word**
part of speech	**related word**	**synonym**	

Name ______________________________ Date ______________

Using a Thesaurus

Directions Look at the sample thesaurus page below. Use it to answer each question.

each • earshot

each *adj.* ***syn*** see ALL.

rel any, several, various; particular, respective, specific

eager *adj.* moved by a strong and urgent desire or interest. (young executives eager to succeed)

syn agog, anxious, appetent, ardent, athirst, avid, breathless, impatient, keen, raring, solicitous, thirsty

rel enthusiastic, gung ho, heated, hot; ambitious, intent, acquisitive, covetous, craving, desirous, hankering

ant listless

earn *v.* to receive as return for effort. (earn a living wage)

syn acquire, bring in, drag down, draw down, gain, get, knock down, make, win

rel attain, effect, obtain, procure, realize, receive, secure

earshot *n.* the range within which something may be heard.

syn hearing, sound

1. What is another word for *eager?* ______________________
2. What is a word that means the opposite of *eager?* ______________________
3. What is a word that is related to *earn?* ______________________
4. What part of speech is *earshot?* ______________________
5. What are the two guide words on this page? ______________________

   Explain what the guide words tell the reader. ______________________

   ____
6. Write a sentence using the synonym for *earshot.* ______________________

   ____

Name ____________________ Date ____________

Show What You Know

Directions Write a five-sentence paragraph describing your best accomplishment. Be sure to use one adjective, or describing word, in each sentence. When you have finished writing your paragraph, read through it and circle your five adjectives.

____

____

____

____

____

____

Directions Write your five circled adjectives in the top row of the chart below. Using a thesaurus, look up each word and find a synonym to replace it. (Remember that the thesaurus can help you find lively words.) Write each word in the second row of the chart.

adjective					
synonym					

Directions Rewrite your paragraph using your new synonyms. Compare the two paragraphs and discuss with a partner which paragraph is better.

____

____

____

____

____

____

Name ______________________ Date ______________

Bibliography Diagram

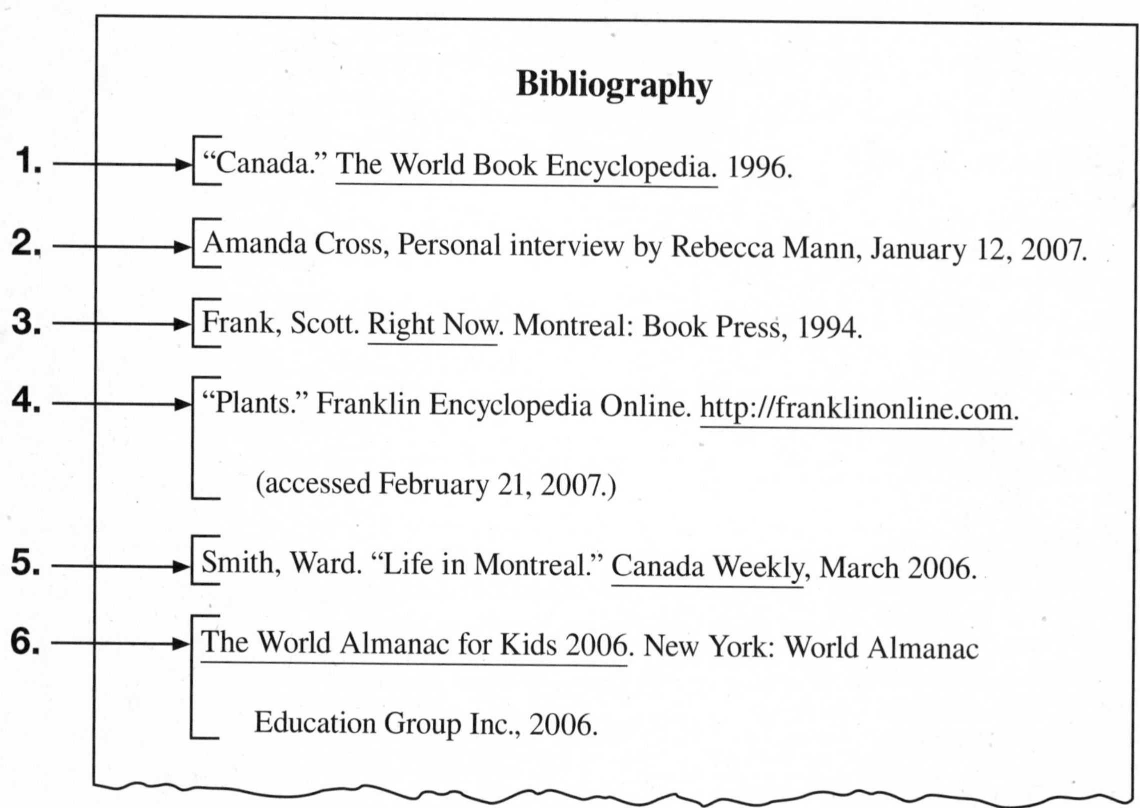

Bibliography
1. "Canada." The World Book Encyclopedia. 1996.
2. Amanda Cross, Personal interview by Rebecca Mann, January 12, 2007.
3. Frank, Scott. Right Now. Montreal: Book Press, 1994.
4. "Plants." Franklin Encyclopedia Online. http://franklinonline.com.
(accessed February 21, 2007.)
5. Smith, Ward. "Life in Montreal." Canada Weekly, March 2006.
6. The World Almanac for Kids 2006. New York: World Almanac
Education Group Inc., 2006.

1. ______________________
2. ______________________
3. ______________________
4. ______________________
5. ______________________
6. ______________________

Name ______________________ Date ____________

Understanding a Bibliography

A **bibliography** is an alphabetical list of the resources used to write a report. A bibliography gives credit to the resources used. Examples of resources include books, magazines, newspapers, Internet documents, almanacs, atlases, encyclopedias, and interviews. Most resources contain the following information.

- author—the person who wrote the resource material
- title—name of the resource or article
- date of publication—year the resource became available to the public
- place of publication—city where the resource was produced

A specific format, or style, should be used when listing each source. The following are commonly used formats.

Book

Author's Last Name, First Name. Title of Book. City of Publication: Name of Publisher, Date of Publication.

Magazine or Newspaper

Author's Last Name, First Name. "Article Title." Magazine or Newspaper Title, Date of Issue.

Internet

Author or Organization. "Title of the work." Internet address. (Date Information Posted or Accessed [if available].)

Almanac & Atlas

Title of Book. City of Publication: Name of Publisher, Date of Publication.

Encyclopedia

"Subject Looked Up." Title of Encyclopedia. Date of Publication.

Interview

First and Last Name of Person Interviewed, Type of Interview (if available) and First and Last Name of Interviewer (if available), Place of Interview (if available).

Directions Look at the bibliography diagram on page 30. Label each part of the diagram.

almanac entry	**book entry**	**encyclopedia entry**
Internet entry	**interview entry**	**magazine entry**

Name ______________________ Date ____________

Using a Bibliography

1. Lasky, Kathryn. The Man Who Made Time Travel. New York: Farrar, Strauss and Giroux, 2003.

2. "New Jersey." Compton's Encyclopedia. 2002.

3. O'Sullivan, Ken. "The Speed of Sound." Odyssey Magazine, March 2006.

4. Neeley, Dandre. "New Skateboard Park Gets a Big Draw." The Record Newspaper, August 21, 1999: NJ1.

5. Arnett, Bill. "Saturn." http://seds.lpl.arizona.edu/nineplanets/nineplanets/saturn.html. (accessed January 26, 2006.)

6. Student World Atlas. New York: Brikman, 2006.

Directions Use the bibliography citations above to complete the table.

	Type of Source	Source Name	Date Published
1.	book		
2.			2002
3.		Odyssey Magazine	
4.	newspaper		
5.		http://seds.lpl.arizona.edu/nineplanets/nineplanets/saturn.html	
6.		Student World Atlas	

Name ______________________________ Date ______________

Show What You Know

Directions Use your school library to find sources on the subject of *super volcanoes.* You should find at least one type of each source, but no more than three of each. Create a bibliography citing the following four types of sources.

- book
- magazine
- encyclopedia
- Internet

Bibliography

____

____

____

____

____

____

____

____

____

____

____

____

____

Directions Record two facts about super volcanoes from each source on another sheet of paper. Write the name of the source next to each fact.

Name ______________________ Date ____________

Understanding a Table of Contents

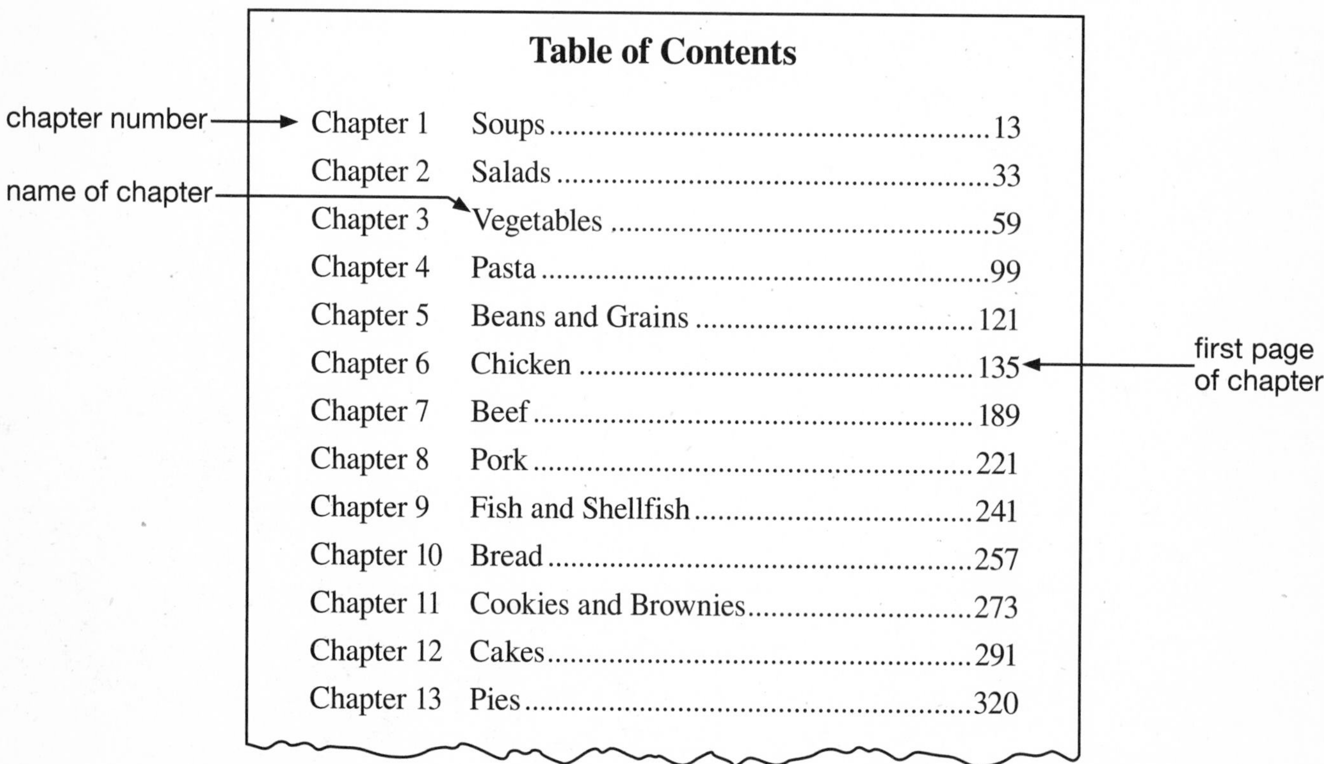

Table of Contents

Chapter	Name	Page
Chapter 1	Soups	13
Chapter 2	Salads	33
Chapter 3	Vegetables	59
Chapter 4	Pasta	99
Chapter 5	Beans and Grains	121
Chapter 6	Chicken	135
Chapter 7	Beef	189
Chapter 8	Pork	221
Chapter 9	Fish and Shellfish	241
Chapter 10	Bread	257
Chapter 11	Cookies and Brownies	273
Chapter 12	Cakes	291
Chapter 13	Pies	320

The **table of contents** is an important feature of a publication, such as a book or magazine. It lists what is in a book.

Each line of the table of contents tells the same kinds of information—the chapter number, the name of the chapter, and the page on which the chapter begins. Chapter names give the reader an idea of what each chapter is about.

Directions Use the table of contents diagram above to answer each question.

1. What kind of book is this table of contents mostly likely from?

____

2. What is the name of the chapter that begins on page 59?

____

3. How many pages are in Chapter 11? ____________________

4. In which chapter would you find a recipe for fried chicken? ____________

Name ______________________ Date ______________

Using a Table of Contents

Directions Use the table of contents below to answer each question.

Table of Contents

1. What is most likely the title of this book? Circle your answer.

Human Settlement   U.S. Geography   World Geography

2. In which chapter can you find information about physical maps?

____

3. How many pages long is Chapter 6? ______________

4. Can you read about the ocean in this book? Explain. ______________

____

5. Can you read about the habitat of bears in this book? Explain. ______________

____

6. If you want to find out what page or pages in the book discuss the topic *weather,* which feature of the book can help you? ______________

7. How many pages are most likely in this book? Circle your answer.

200   96   150

8. What will pages 10 and 11 be about? ______________

Using Information Resources 4, SV 9781419099397

Name ______________________________ Date ______________

Show What You Know

Directions You have been assigned to write a short book with five chapters on frogs. **1.** Go to the library and research information on frogs. **2.** Brainstorm the five most important topics below. **3.** Use the information from your web to create a table of contents for your book. **4.** Write your table of contents in the space below the web. Remember to give it a title. Also include at least one features page in your table of contents.

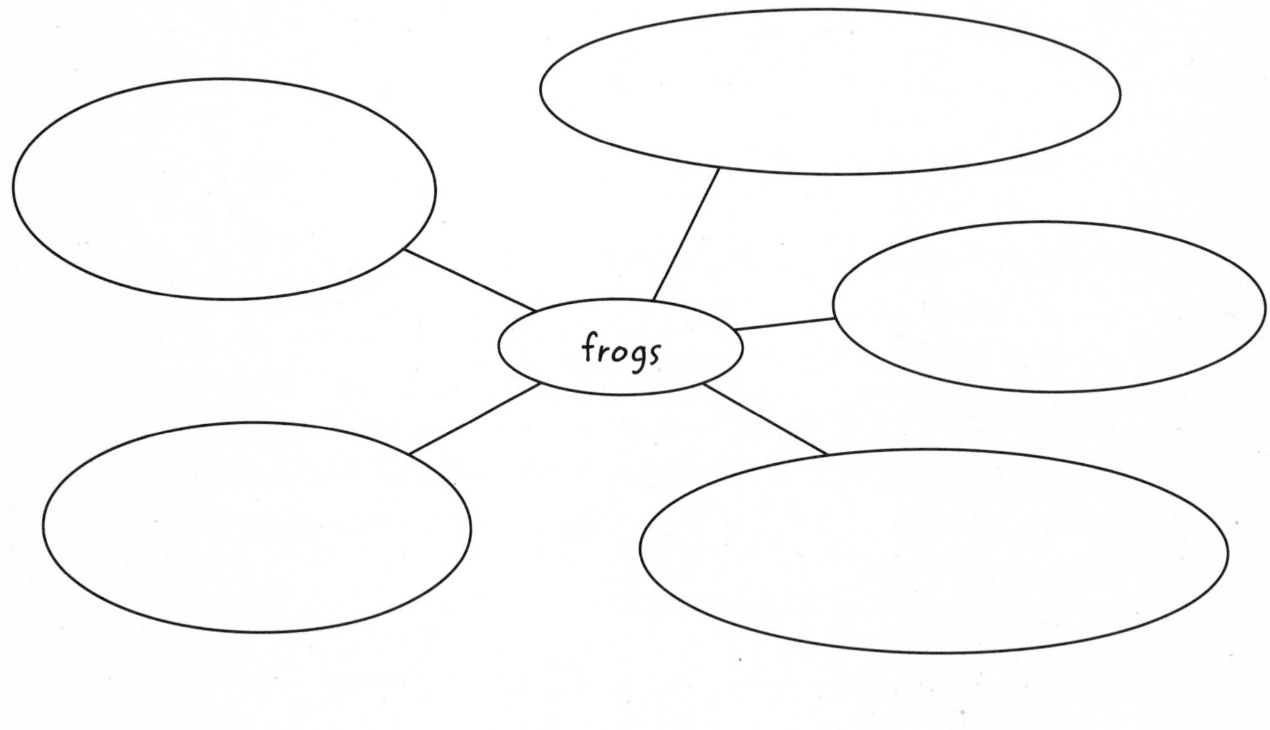

____

Name ________________________ Date ____________

Understanding Headings and Captions

Chapter 3: All About Mammals

heading → **Introducing Mammals**

Most of the animals we have as pets, like dogs, cats, and horses, are mammals. Humans are also mammals. Mammals belong to a group of animals known as vertebrates. Vertebrates have a backbone and they are warmblooded. Most mammals have hair or fur on their bodies. They give birth to live young and feed them with milk. Because mammals are warmblooded, they can survive in almost any environment.

The kangaroo is a pouched mammal, known as a marsupial. ← caption

When reading an article or a page in a nonfiction book, the reader can skim through the information to get an idea of what it is about. This means quickly looking over the text to get an overview of its contents. When the reader uses a resource to answer questions or find information, he or she can scan, or examine, the text to find specific information.

Looking at **headings** and **captions** is a good way to find out what information is covered in the text. Headings tell what the text beneath them will be about. The reader will learn the details from the text. Captions are words or sentences next to a picture that tell about it. The information in a caption is important because it might not be anywhere else in the text.

Directions Use the heading and captions diagram above to answer each question.

1. What does the heading suggest the paragraph will be about? ____________

   ____

2. What information does the caption tell about the picture that you would not know from the sentences? ____________

Name ______________________ Date ____________

Using Headings and Captions

Directions Read the information below. Write headings for each section. Then write a caption for each illustration.

Chapter 3: Firefighters

Firefighters are men and women who risk their lives every day to protect the community. Fires are one of the most serious dangers that can threaten a city or town.

1. Heading: ______________________

Fire departments are divided into *companies.* Each company has quarters in a neighborhood fire station. Big-city fire stations have large crews of firefighters standing by at all times, ready to respond to an alarm. Volunteer firefighters protect small cities and rural communities. They do not earn their living fighting fires. When there is an emergency, they rush from their work or their home to the fire station.

2. Caption: ______________________

3. Heading: ______________________

Firefighters need special tools to do their jobs. Some everyday tools have been changed to meet the needs of firefighters. A fire axe helps the firefighter break down doors and chop holes in walls and roofs. A rope hose tool is used to secure a hose to a ladder and to tie victims to the firefighter's back. A searchlight helps firefighters work in the dark. Crowbars are useful for opening windows and prying open floorboards.

4. Caption: ______________________

Directions In the space below, create another illustration that could be used with the information above. Then write a caption to go with the picture.

5. Caption: ______________________

Name ______________________ Date ______________

Show What You Know

Directions **1.** Open your science or social studies book to a page that includes a heading and a caption. Read the heading. In the chart below, write what you predict the section will be about in the first column. **2.** Look at the illustration and then read the caption. Make another prediction, in the second column, on what the section will be about. **3.** Now scan the text on the page for keywords and information, such as vocabulary. Record this information in the third column of the chart. **4.** Read the page and record what the text is mostly about in the fourth column of the chart. **5.** Record in the last column any new and interesting information you learned and write whether your predictions were correct.

My prediction after reading the heading	My prediction after looking at the illustration and reading the caption	Keywords and information I found from scanning	What the text is mostly about	What I learned and if my predictions were correct

Directions After completing the chart, think about why reading headings and captions is important. Also think about how scanning text and previewing illustrations can help you. Explain why this skill and these features are important.

____

____

____

____

Name ______________________ Date ____________

Understanding an Index

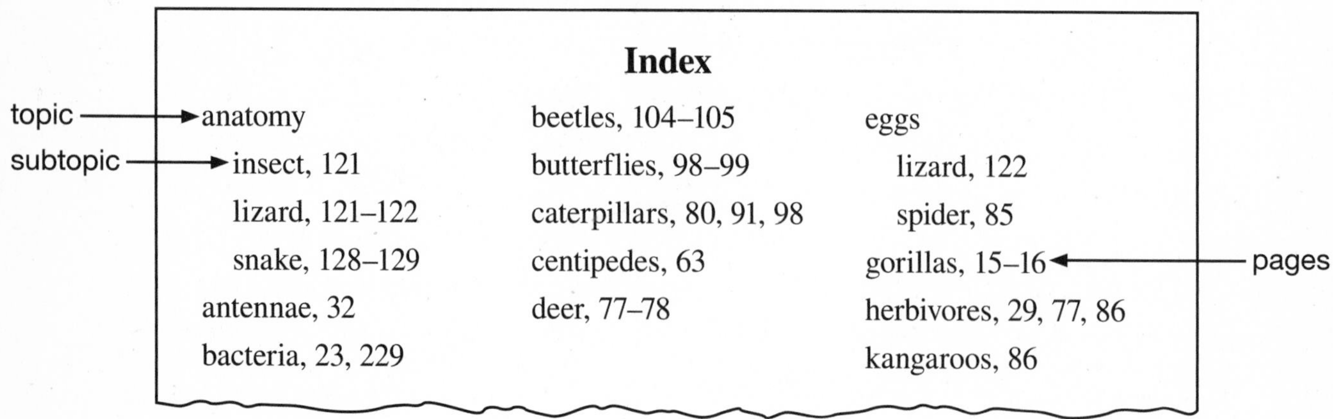

The **index** is found in the back of a book. It lists many topics from the book in alphabetical order. Sometimes a topic has subtopics, or more detailed topics. For instance, if the topic in the index is *sports,* subtopics might be *basketball, football, golf,* and *soccer.* An index is used to find the pages that have information about a certain topic.

Directions Use the index diagram above to answer each question.

1. In what order are the topics in the index? ____________
2. On what page or pages can you learn about swallowtail butterflies?

   ____
3. What two topics are on page 86? ____________
4. What can you learn about on pages 80, 91, and 98? ____________
5. Do you think you can learn about bacteria in more than one chapter? ______

   Why or why not? ____________

   ____

Name ______________________________ Date ______________

Using an Index

Directions Use the index to answer each question.

Index

1. What would be the best title for the book in which this index is found? Circle your answer.

   Using Nouns   How to Spell Well   Rules for Good Writing

2. Is this book fiction or nonfiction? ______________

3. What page would you turn to if you need to learn how to edit? ______________

4. How many subtopics does the topic *Capitalization* have? ______________

5. Looking at the subtopics for page 5, what is the page mostly about?

   ____

6. What page would you turn to if you need to read about the rule for words that end in consonant letters? ______________

7. What can you learn about on pages 18 and 19? ______________

8. If you want to check whether to use the word *meat* instead of *meet* in your sentence, what section should you turn to? ______________

Name ______________________ Date ____________

Show What You Know

Directions Find a book that has an index. Use it to answer each question and to follow the directions.

1. What is the title of the book? ______________________
2. How many pages are included in the book? ______________________
3. What is one topic listed in the index? ______________________
4. What page or pages can you read to learn about that topic? ______________________
5. Go to a page about that topic. Write down three facts from that page.

   ____
6. What is the first topic in the index? ______________________
7. What is the last topic in the index? ______________________
8. What are the page numbers of the last topic listed in the index?

   ____
9. Write one subtopic and the topic it falls under.

   topic: ______________________ subtopic: ______________________
10. Locate a topic in the index that looks interesting. Go to the page or pages about that topic. Write down any headings and captions on those pages. Also write down what visual features, such as maps, graphs, or time lines, are included. Write a short paragraph explaining how the index is helpful to you.

    Headings and Captions: ______________________

    ____

    ____

    Visual features: ______________________

    ____

    ____

    Paragraph: ______________________

    ____

    ____

Name ______________________ Date ______________

Understanding a Glossary

Glossary of Spanish Words

adiós goodbye
aficionado an intense enthusiast; a fan
churros Mexican fried dough
fiesta a party or celebration
hacienda an estate or a ranch
loco mad or crazy
nopalitos cooked strips from the fleshy leaf of the prickly pear tree
playa beach
quesadilla a hot, flat sandwich made of tortillas and melted cheese
siesta a short nap taken in the early afternoon
queso cheese
taco tortilla stuffed with meat or other filling
tamales Mexican stuffed dumplings made of cornmeal wrapped in corn husks and steamed
tortillas flat, round pancakes made of corn or wheat flour
turista tourist

A **glossary** is a list of words and their meanings, usually listed in alphabetical order. The glossary is often found in the back of a book. Words found in the book that are necessary and uncommon are included in the glossary. Previewing the words in a glossary can help the reader to better comprehend text.

Directions Look at the glossary. Use it to help you write a sentence for each word below. Write your sentences on the lines.

1. tamales ______________________________

2. siesta ______________________________

3. quesadillas ______________________________

4. adiós ______________________________

5. fiesta ______________________________

Name ______________________ Date ______________

Using a Glossary

Glossary

solar system a group of objects in space that move around a star (p. 92)

solid the state of matter that has a definite shape and takes up a definite amount of space (p. 6)

species a group of similar organisms that can reproduce (p. 68)

speed the distance an object moves divided by the time during which it moves (p. 18)

star a glowing ball of gas (p. 92)

static electricity a charge that does not flow (p. 30)

thermal energy the total energy of the particles in a sample of matter (p. 30)

tissue a group of cells that work together to perform a task (p. 44)

translucent relating to an object that reflects some light, absorbs some light, and transmits some light (p. 30)

transparent relating to an object that allows light to pass through (p. 30)

volume the amount of space an object or material takes up (p. 7)

weathering the process through which natural forces, such as wind and water, break down rocks and other materials into smaller pieces (p. 80)

122

Directions Use the glossary to answer each question.

1. What subject do the entry words in this glossary cover? ______________
2. How many entries are on this sample glossary page? ______________
3. If you read the definition for the entry words *thermal energy* and still are unsure what this term means, what information is given that can help you to learn more about the entry words? ______________
4. Based on the definitions provided, what is the difference between *translucent* and *transparent?* ______________
5. Read the definitions for *solar system* and *star.* How are the two words related? ______________

Name ______________________ Date ____________

Show What You Know

Directions Use a book that has a glossary to answer each question and to follow the directions.

1. What is the name of the book the glossary appears in? ____________

2. How many terms in the glossary start with the letter *p*? ____________

3. Which term is listed last? ____________

4. Which term is listed first? ____________

5. List three words that are new to you and their meanings.

____

____

____

6. How many pages are in the glossary? ____________

7. Choose two words from the glossary and write two sentences using them. Use one sentence for each word.

____

____

____

____

8. Think about how the glossary is helpful to you. Describe how you can use glossaries in the future as a resource.

____

____

____

____

____

____

Name ______________________ Date ____________

Table Diagram

1. → **Animal Names** ← 2.

3. →

Animal	Male	Female	Young	Group Name
bear	boar	sow	cub	sleuth, sloth
cat	tom	queen	kitten	clutter, clowder
chicken	rooster	hen	chick	brood, clutch
deer	buck	doe	fawn	herd, leash
duck	drake	duck	duckling	brace, team
elephant	bull	cow	calf	herd
fox	dog	vixen	cub	leash, skulk
goose	gander	goose	gosling	flock, gaggle, skein
horse	stallion	mare	foal	pair, team
lion	lion	lioness	cub	pride
pig	boar	sow	piglet	litter
sheep	ram	ewe	lamb	drove, flock
swan	cob	pen	cygnet	bevy, wedge

4. → (elephant row)

1. ______________________
2. ______________________
3. ______________________
4. ______________________

Name ______________________________ Date ____________

Understanding a Table

Tables are a useful way to present information. The **title** is at the top of the table. It tells the topic of the information given in the table. The information is arranged by **rows** and **columns.** The rows are the lines that go across. The columns are the lines that go up and down.

In a table, the **column heading,** or word at the top of the column, tells what information is given in that column. It helps to better understand how the information is organized.

Directions Use the table diagram on page 46 to complete each sentence.

1. A boar is a male ______________.
2. The ______________ of chicks chased after their mother.
3. The ______________ provided milk to her foal.
4. The female elephant is a ______________ and her baby is a ______________.
5. The lion stuck with the big group, called a ______________.
6. The sow took very good care of her ______________ of piglets.
7. A group of cygnets is called a ______________.
8. The mother ewe looked for her ______________ of lambs.

Directions Look at the table diagram on page 46. Use the words below to label the diagram.

column	**column heading**	**row**	**title**

Name ______________________________ Date ______________

Using a Table

Directions Use the table below to answer each question.

U.S. Paper Money		
Bill	**Front Portrait**	**Design on Back**
$1	Washington	The word *One* between images of the Great Seal of the United States
$2	Jefferson	The signing of the Declaration of Independence
$5	Lincoln	Lincoln Memorial Building
$10	Hamilton	U.S. Treasury Building
$20	Jackson	The White House
$50	Grant	The U.S. Capitol
$100	Franklin	Independence Hall in Philadelphia

1. Who is on the front of the $100 bill? ______________________

2. What is on the back of the $2 bill? ______________________

3. How many columns are in the table? ______________________

4. What is the title of the table? ______________________

5. How many different bills are listed? ______________________

6. Who is on the front of the $20 bill? ______________________

7. How many bills have buildings as part of the design on back? __________

8. What are the three column headings?

____

9. What do all the designs on the back of the paper money have in common?

____

10. What type of resource might you find this table in? Explain.

____

____

Name ____________________ Date ____________

Show What You Know

Directions Talk to five students in your class. Find out about how much time they spend reading and watching television each day. Create a table to show the data you collect and give your table a name. The column headings should be *Name, Time Spent Reading,* and *Time Spent Watching Television.*

____

______________	______________ ______________	______________ ______________
1.		
2.		
3.		
4.		
5.		

Directions Write four questions that can be answered by looking at the table. Trade papers with a partner and answer the questions. Check to see that he or she answered your questions correctly.

6. Question: ______________________________

Answer: ______________________________

7. Question: ______________________________

Answer: ______________________________

8. Question: ______________________________

Answer: ______________________________

9. Question: ______________________________

Answer: ______________________________

Name ______________________ Date ______________

Schedule Diagrams

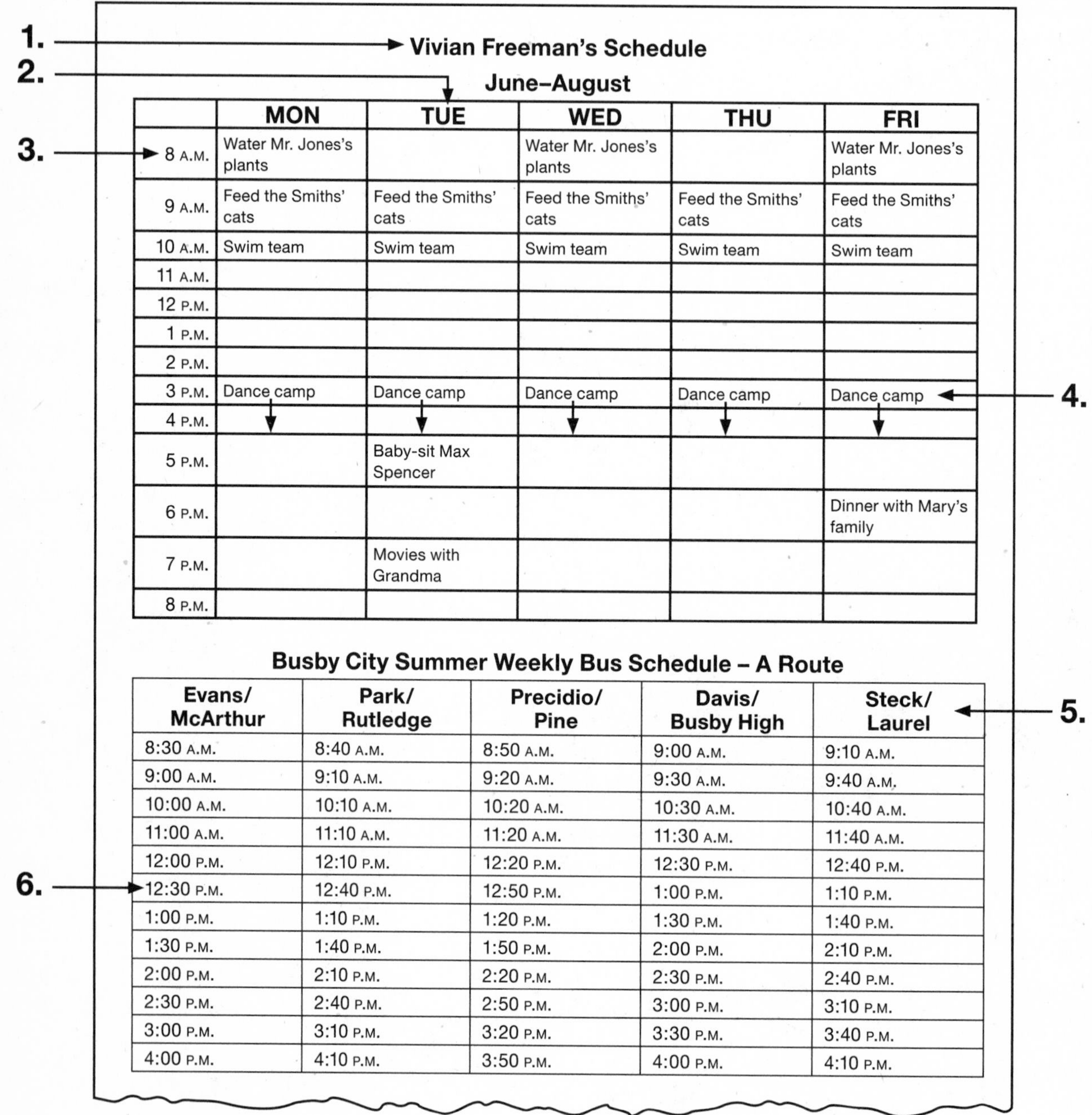

1. → **Vivian Freeman's Schedule**
2. → **June–August**

3. →	MON	TUE	WED	THU	FRI
8 A.M.	Water Mr. Jones's plants		Water Mr. Jones's plants		Water Mr. Jones's plants
9 A.M.	Feed the Smiths' cats	Feed the Smiths' cats	Feed the Smiths' cats	Feed the Smiths' cats	Feed the Smiths' cats
10 A.M.	Swim team	Swim team	Swim team	Swim team	Swim team
11 A.M.					
12 P.M.					
1 P.M.					
2 P.M.					
3 P.M.	Dance camp	Dance camp	Dance camp	Dance camp	Dance camp ← 4.
4 P.M.	↓	↓	↓	↓	↓
5 P.M.		Baby-sit Max Spencer			
6 P.M.					Dinner with Mary's family
7 P.M.		Movies with Grandma			
8 P.M.					

Busby City Summer Weekly Bus Schedule – A Route

Evans/ McArthur	Park/ Rutledge	Precidio/ Pine	Davis/ Busby High	Steck/ Laurel ← 5.
8:30 A.M.	8:40 A.M.	8:50 A.M.	9:00 A.M.	9:10 A.M.
9:00 A.M.	9:10 A.M.	9:20 A.M.	9:30 A.M.	9:40 A.M.
10:00 A.M.	10:10 A.M.	10:20 A.M.	10:30 A.M.	10:40 A.M.
11:00 A.M.	11:10 A.M.	11:20 A.M.	11:30 A.M.	11:40 A.M.
12:00 P.M.	12:10 P.M.	12:20 P.M.	12:30 P.M.	12:40 P.M.
6. → 12:30 P.M.	12:40 P.M.	12:50 P.M.	1:00 P.M.	1:10 P.M.
1:00 P.M.	1:10 P.M.	1:20 P.M.	1:30 P.M.	1:40 P.M.
1:30 P.M.	1:40 P.M.	1:50 P.M.	2:00 P.M.	2:10 P.M.
2:00 P.M.	2:10 P.M.	2:20 P.M.	2:30 P.M.	2:40 P.M.
2:30 P.M.	2:40 P.M.	2:50 P.M.	3:00 P.M.	3:10 P.M.
3:00 P.M.	3:10 P.M.	3:20 P.M.	3:30 P.M.	3:40 P.M.
4:00 P.M.	4:10 P.M.	3:50 P.M.	4:00 P.M.	4:10 P.M.

1. ______________________ 4. ______________________

2. ______________________ 5. ______________________

3. ______________________ 6. ______________________

Name ____________________ Date ____________

Understanding a Schedule

Vivian Freeman has a busy summer schedule during the weekdays. She does various jobs for neighbors to earn extra money. She also keeps busy with dance camp and swim team. She has to keep a daily schedule so she doesn't forget anything. She also has to keep track of the local bus schedule in order to ride the city bus to dance camp at the high school across town.

A **schedule** is a helpful tool that is a type of chart or table. It is usually organized into rows and columns to help readers use its content. It lists **times** and **days** that appointments, jobs, and other **activities** will happen. The top schedule on page 50 lists a day of the week for each column heading. Each row lists a time of day. The **title** of the schedule tells for whom or what the schedule is written. The title might also include the time period the schedule covers.

The bottom schedule on page 50 lists the **departure times** for each **bus stop** on a certain route.

Directions Look at the schedule diagram on page 50. Use the words below to label it.

activity	bus stop	day	departure time	time	title

Name ______________________________ Date ______________

Using a Schedule

Directions Vivian often gets calls from other neighbors during the summer to do work for them. She also tries to spend time with her friends. Below are five more activities Vivian needs to fit into her busy schedule. Add each activity to Vivian's schedule on page 50.

1. On Monday, Marissa will come over at 6 P.M. to watch a movie. Marissa has to leave at 8 P.M.
2. Vivian is going to baby-sit Max Spencer again on Thursday from 6 P.M.–7 P.M.
3. Vivian will walk the Roarks' dog for one hour on Tuesday and Thursday mornings at 8 A.M.
4. On Wednesday at 1 P.M., Vivian is going with Joey Smith to the library.
5. Vivian's friend Jake wants to meet on Monday at 4 P.M., Wednesday at 11 A.M., or Thursday at 12 P.M. Which time works for Vivian? Schedule their meeting.

Directions Use the schedules on page 50 to answer each question.

6. What does Vivian need to do on Monday, Wednesday, and Friday mornings?

   ____

7. How long does dance camp last each day? ______________
8. On Friday, how much time does Vivian have between dance camp and dinner at Mary's house? ______________
9. What three tasks does Vivian have every day?

   ____

10. What day does Vivian get to see Grandma? ______________
11. If Vivian wants to plan an evening to see her old friend Margie, what nights is she available? ______________
12. Which bus route does Vivian take to dance camp? ______________
13. If Vivian's bus pickup is Park/Rutledge and her destination is Davis/Busby High, what time does she need to catch the bus to be on time for dance camp?

    ____

Name ______________________ Date ____________

Show What You Know

Directions Use a TV program schedule from your local newspaper to answer each question.

1. What does the schedule show? ______________________

____

2. How is the schedule organized? ______________________

____

3. What are three television programs that will be aired at 3:00 P.M. on Tuesday?

____

____

4. What is a movie that will be aired at 8:00 P.M. on Friday? ______________________
5. Do you notice any programs that air daily? If so, list one program's name and the time it airs. ______________________
6. What is the name of a sports program and the time that it will be aired on Monday? ______________________
7. How many television channels are shown on the schedule? ______________________
8. What special symbols are shown on the schedule? ______________________

Directions With a partner, plan a weekly schedule on another sheet of paper for a new television channel. Be sure to label the schedule and include titles and special symbols that will allow the reader to understand what is showing. Plan four interesting facts about the schedule to share with the class.

Name ______________________ Date ____________

Graph Diagrams

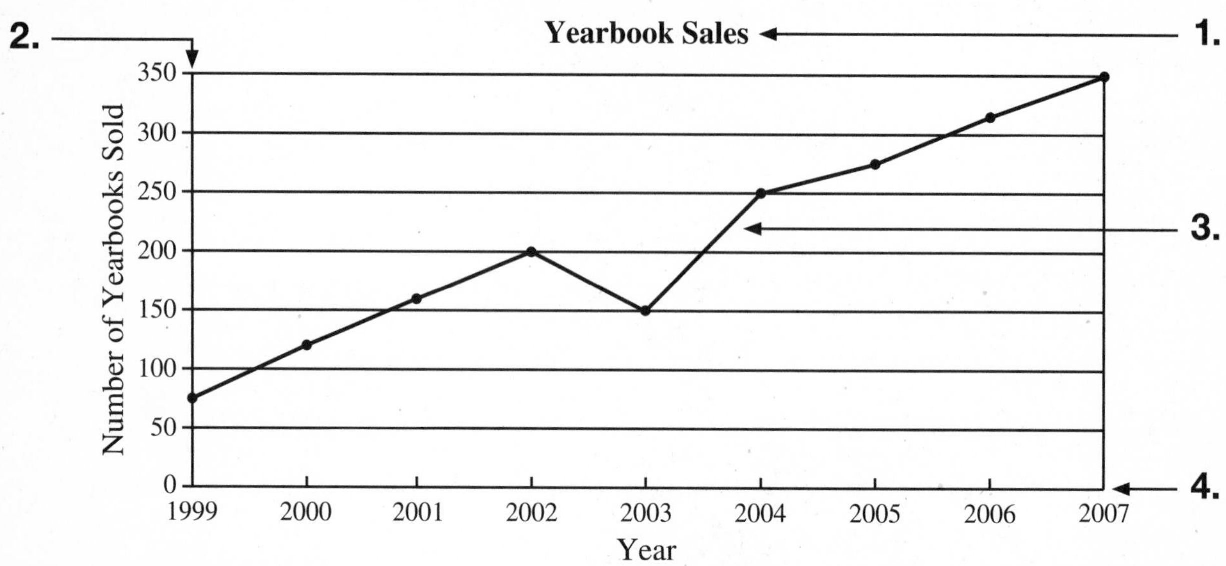

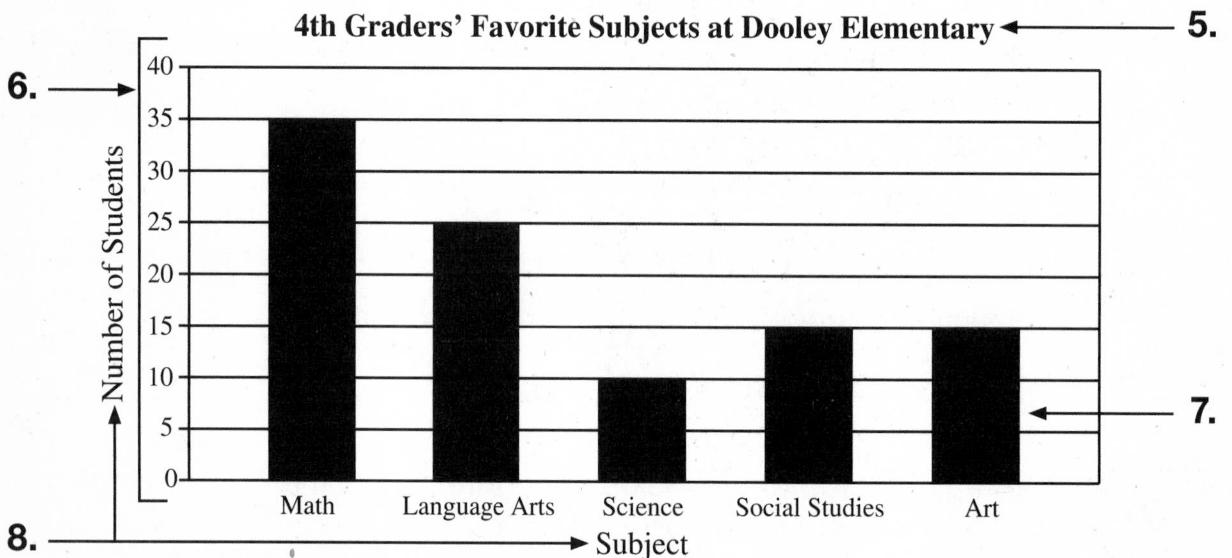

1. ______________________ 5. ______________________

2. ______________________ 6. ______________________

3. ______________________ 7. ______________________

4. ______________________ 8. ______________________

Name ______________________________ Date ______________

Understanding Graphs

A **graph** is a drawing that shows information in a way that is easy to understand and compare.

A **line graph** is a type of graph that uses a **line** to show trends or a change in numbers over a period of time.

- The **title** tells what the graph shows.
- The ***y*-axis,** or vertical axis, goes up and down on the left side of the graph.
- The ***x*-axis,** or horizontal axis, goes left to right across the bottom.
- The **line graph labels** explain the information. In this case, the labels go up the *y*-axis and across the *x*-axis.

A **bar graph** is a type of graph that uses bars to show how different things compare to one another at the same time.

- The **bar graph labels** on a bar graph explain the information. On the graph, the labels at the side tell how many. The labels across the bottom tell what the bars represent.
- The **scale** shows the range of numbers represented on the graph.
- The **bars** stand for numbers.

Directions Use the words below to help you label the graph diagrams on page 54.

bar	**bar graph title**	**labels**	**line**
line graph title	**scale**	***x*-axis**	***y*-axis**

Name ______________________ Date ____________

Using Graphs

Directions Use the line graph on page 54 to answer each question.

1. What year were the fewest yearbooks sold? ____________
2. What year were the most yearbooks sold? ____________
3. How many more yearbooks were sold in 2004 than 2003? ____________
4. In what year was there a drop in sales? ____________
5. How many years does the graph show? ____________
6. For the most part, did yearbook sales grow or decline? ____________
7. How do you think this information could be useful? ____________

____

____

Directions Use the bar graph on page 54 to answer each question.

8. What does the graph show? ____________
9. What is the most popular subject? ____________
10. How many students like art best? ____________
11. What is the second-favorite subject? ____________
12. What is the least-popular subject? ____________
13. How many more students prefer math than science? ____________
14. Which two subjects are preferred by the same number of students?

    ____

15. How many students in all does the graph show? ____________

Name ______________________ Date ______________

Show What You Know

Mrs. Johnson conducted a survey to find out what kind of pets the students in her class have. She found the following information:

No Pet—6
Dog—7
Cat—6
Fish—2
Other—2

Directions Use the space below to create a bar graph that will correctly show Mrs. Johnson's class information. Give the graph a title and labels. On another sheet of paper, write three questions that can be answered by reading your graph. Trade papers with a partner and answer the questions. Check to make sure the answers are correct.

Name ______________________ Date ______________

Time Line

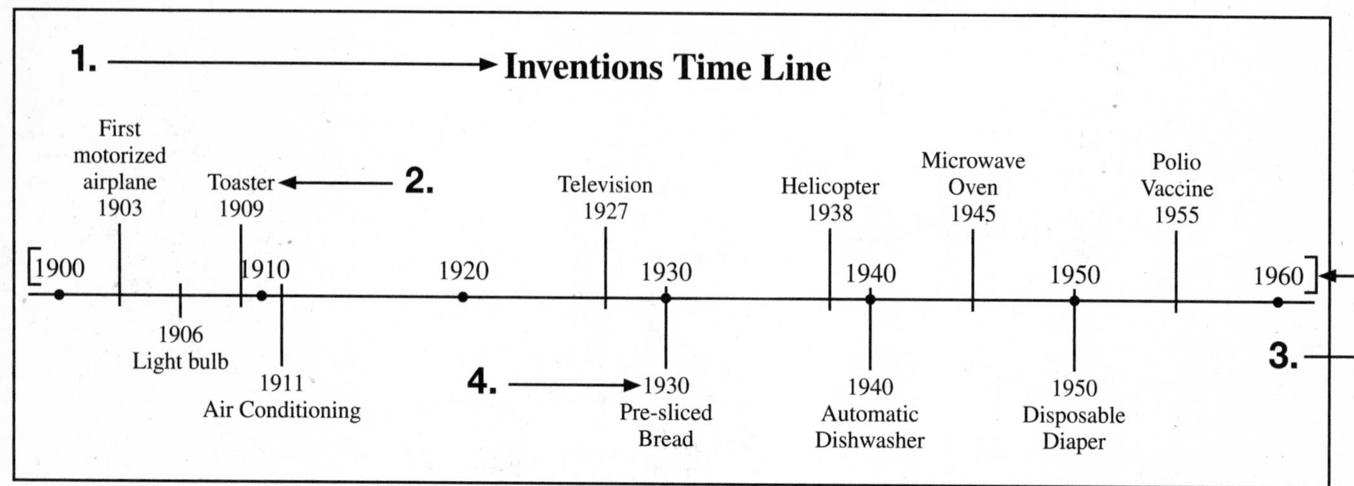

1.
Inventions Time Line
First motorized airplane 1903
Toaster 1909
2.
Television 1927
Helicopter 1938
Microwave Oven 1945
Polio Vaccine 1955
1900
1910
1920
1930
1940
1950
1960
1906 Light bulb
1911 Air Conditioning
4.
1930 Pre-sliced Bread
1940 Automatic Dishwasher
1950 Disposable Diaper
3.

1. ______________________

2. ______________________

3. ______________________

4. ______________________

Name ______________________________ Date ______________

Understanding a Time Line

A **time line** is a visual tool that shows **events** in the sequence, or order, that they happened. Time lines are useful for showing important events in someone's life or showing one topic over time.

The **title** of the time line tells what information is being given. The time line shows **dates,** or specific points in time. The **period of time** shows a range of time between the first and last dates. Important events are labeled within this range.

Directions Look at the time line on page 58. Use it to answer each question.

1. What is the time line about? ______________________________
2. In what year was the light bulb invented? ______________________________
3. What was invented in 1930? ______________________________
4. How many years after the invention of air conditioning was the disposable diaper introduced? ______________________________
5. How many years in all are represented on the time line? ______________________________
6. According to the time line, which ten-year period had the most inventions?

   ____

Directions Look at the time line diagram on page 58. Use the words below to label the time line.

date	**event**	**period of time**	**title**

Name ______________________ Date ____________

Using a Time Line

Directions Use the time line below to answer the questions.

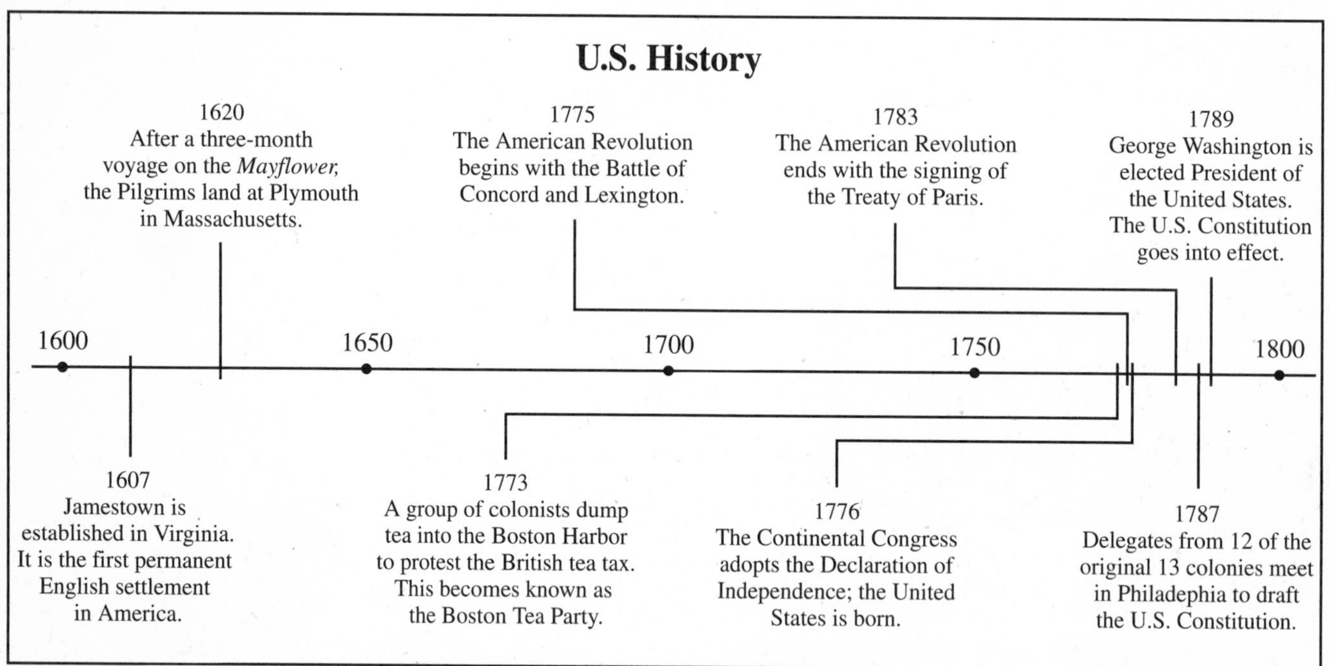

1. What happened in 1620? ______________________

____

2. When did the American Revolution begin? ______________________

3. When did the American Revolution end? ______________________

4. When did George Washington become president? ______________________

5. What else happened in the same year George Washington became president?

____

6. When was the Boston Tea Party? ______________________

7. How long was the Pilgrims' voyage on the *Mayflower?* ______________________

8. What might be a better title for the time line? Circle your answer.

   U.S. War History   Early U.S. History   History of Tea

9. When did the United States become an official country? ______________________

10. How many years passed between the first American settlement and the creation of the United States? ______________________

Name ______________________________ Date ______________

Show What You Know

Directions On another sheet of paper, make a time line to show the historical information included in the paragraph below. The years on the time line should be 1945, 1955, 1960, 1965, and 1970. Put the events in the correct order on the time line. Give the time line a title.

Many important events happened in U.S. history after World War II. In 1954, the U.S. Supreme Court ruled that segregation by race in public schools was unconstitutional. During that same year, a polio vaccination was introduced to immunize people against the deadly disease. One year later, a key event in the civil rights movement occurred when Rosa Parks refused to give up her seat on a city bus. John F. Kennedy was elected President of the United States in 1960 and began a program called The New Frontier. In 1963, President Kennedy was assassinated, and Vice President Lyndon B. Johnson became president. During that same year, Martin Luther King, Jr., delivered his "I have a dream . . ." speech. President Johnson was elected to serve a full term as president, and troops were sent to Vietnam in 1964. Martin Luther King, Jr., was assassinated in 1968. In that same year, Richard M. Nixon was elected president. The United States sent the first humans to the moon in 1969, and the Vietnam War ended in 1973. President Nixon resigned as president, and Vice President Gerald R. Ford became president in 1974.

Directions Write three questions that can be answered by looking at your time line. Then answer each question.

Question 1: ______________________________

Answer: ______________________________

Question 2: ______________________________

Answer: ______________________________

Question 3: ______________________________

Answer: ______________________________

Answer Key

Page 3
1. guide words
2. entry word
3. sample sentence
4. raised number
5. pronunciation guide
6. definition
7. part of speech
8. definition number
9. page number

Page 5
1. Eskimos, places, world
2. Alaska, state, United States
3. communities, Greenland, Canada
4. people, temperatures
5. Eskimos, Arctic, polar bears
6. hunters, walruses
7. animals, meat, tusks
8. material, knives, hooks, tools
9. centuries, Eskimos, ice, sea, water
10. language, speech, Native Americans
11. Eskimos, homes
12. buildings, igloos

Page 6
1. He
2. We
3. them
4. They
5. them
6. us
7. them
8. it
9. we
10. Answers will vary.

Page 7
1. 4; injured
2. 3; good
3. 1; kind
4. 5; poor
5. 6; soft
6. 2; grateful, strong
7. Correct sentence order: 4, 3, 1, 5, 6, 2

Page 8
Answers will vary. Possible answers include the following:
1. lives
2. moved
3. seems
4. flew
5. appeared
6. roared
7. looked
8. was
9. were
10. ate
11. tasted
12. slept

Page 9
Answers will vary. Possible answers include the following:
1. excitedly
2. tomorrow
3. happily
4. quickly
5. carefully
6. Here
7. busily
8. slowly
9. finally
10. wearily
11. quietly
12. upstairs

Page 10
1. The word *doesn't* should be underlined; does not
2. The word *isn't* should be underlined; is not
3. The word *hasn't* should be underlined; has not
4. The word *isn't* should be underlined; is not
5. The word *doesn't* should be underlined; does not
6. The word *wouldn't* should be underlined; would not
7. The word *weren't* should be underlined; were not
8. The word *don't* should be underlined; do not
9. The word *haven't* should be underlined; have not
10. The word *shouldn't* should be underlined; should not

Page 11
1. unfair
2. returned
3. unable
4. misunderstood
5. preplanned
6. impatiently
7. repay
8. unhappy
9. displeased
10. returned

Page 12
1. The word *stormy* should be circled; what kind
2. The word *visitor* should be circled; one who
3. The word *politely* should be circled; how
4. The word *musical* should be circled; like
5. The word *wonderful* should be circled; full of
6. The word *magical* should be circled; like
7. The word *unforgettable* should be circled; able to be
8. The word *unbelievable* should be circled; able to be
9. The word *storyteller* should be circled; one who

Page 13
1. The word *parka* should be circled; 2
2. The word *snow* should be circled; 1
3. The word *machine* should be circled; 2
4. The word *caribou* should be circled; 3
5. The word *father* should be circled; 2
6. The word *surprise* should be circled; 2
7. The word *light* should be circled; 1
8. The word *design* should be circled; 2

Page 14
Sentences will vary. Possible sentences include the following:
1. There is no lead in the pencil.
2. The yarn is wound around my finger.
3. The pizza did not last long.
4. Is that a tear in your eye?
5. Please close the door.

Homograph lists will vary.

Page 15
1. The words *anxious, amount, arrest, alive, also,* and *ant* should be circled.
2. The words *fourth, flower, fog, fly, flame, flew,* and *flight* should be circled.
3. The words *side, shawl, seventeen, sink, settle, sign,* and *shelter* should be circled.
4. The words in alphabetical order are *lamp, last, late, lawn;* guide words are *lamp* and *lawn.*
5. The words in alphabetical order are *pad, page, palm, pass;* guide words are *pad* and *pass.*

Page 16
1. member, mine
2. 7
3. verb
4. mere
5. 1
6. migration
7. migrate
8. no
9. meteor
10. Answers will vary.

Page 17
Answers will vary for 1–5. Ensure each possible answer includes a reasonable clue. Possible answers include the following:
1. done skillfully and tastefully
2. an art form in which various small objects are pasted together on a surface
3. having or showing imagination and artistic ability
4. a particular way of looking at a situation
5. something carved out of stone, wood, metal, marble, or clay, or cast out of bronze or another metal

Paragraphs will vary.

Page 18
1. title
2. city of publication
3. year published
4. author
5. publishing company
6. call number

Page 20
1. *Tyrannosaurus Rex, Deltadromeus: Facts and Photos*
2. Education Publishers
3. Select the book from the list to get more information.
4. A title search is the best type of search.
5. Subjects include fairies, magic, and adventure.

Page 21
1.–5. Answers will vary
6. You can find more books by doing an author search.
7. Answers will vary. Ensure chart is completed.

Page 22
1. coordinates
2. page number
3. place
4. line of longitude
5. position point
6. scale
7. line of latitude
8. compass rose
9. legend

Page 24
1. page 75
2. E-5
3. 74
4. southwest
5. Red River
6. Austin
7. Gulf of Mexico
8. west
9. Houston
10. Rio Grande
11. Austin
12. C-2 and D-2

Page 25
1.–4. Answers will vary.
5. Brazil
6. India
7. Answers will vary.
8. Great Salt Lake
9. Questions and answers will vary.

Page 26
1. guide words
2. entry word
3. part of speech
4. synonym
5. definition
6. antonym
7. related word

Page 27
1. two
2. perform, permeable
3. Answers may include safety or security.
4. Answers will vary. *Sample answer:* It helps make it easier to find an entry on the page.
5. no

Page 28
1. Answers will vary. *Sample answer:* anxious
2. listless
3. Answers will vary. *Sample answer:* attain
4. noun
5. each, earshot; answers will vary.
6. Sentences will vary.

Page 29
Answers will vary.

Page 30
1. encyclopedia entry
2. interview entry
3. book entry
4. Internet entry
5. magazine entry
6. almanac entry

Page 32
1. <u>The Man Who Made Time Travel</u>; 2003
2. encyclopedia; <u>Compton's Encyclopedia</u>
3. magazine; March 2006
4. <u>The Record Newspaper</u>; August 21, 1999
5. Internet; January 26, 2006
6. atlas; 2006

Page 33
Answers will vary.

Page 34
1. cookbook
2. Vegetables
3. 18
4. Chapter 6

Page 35
1. <u>World Geography</u>
2. Chapter 2
3. 20 pages
4. Yes, Chapter 4 talks about water. The ocean is a body of water.
5. No, this book does not cover bears or their habitats.
6. index
7. 96
8. geography

Page 36
Answers will vary.

Page 37
1. Answers will vary. *Sample answer:* The heading suggests the paragraph will be an introduction to mammals.
2. The caption tells that the kangaroo is a marsupial and has a pouch.

Page 38
Answers will vary.

Page 39
Answers will vary.

Page 40
1. alphabetical
2. 98–99
3. herbivores, kangaroos
4. caterpillars
5. Answers will vary. *Sample answer:* Yes, because the pages listed are far apart

Page 41
1. <u>Rules for Good Writing</u>
2. nonfiction
3. page 45
4. 18
5. capitalizing proper nouns
6. page 42
7. apostrophes
8. Commonly Misused Words

Page 42
Answers will vary.

Page 43
Sentences will vary.

Page 44
1. science
2. 12
3. page number that has text on the topic
4. Answers will vary. *Sample answer:* A transparent object allows light to pass through, but a translucent object lets only some light pass through. The rest is absorbed or reflected.
5. The solar system moves around a star.

Page 45
Answers will vary.

Page 46
1. title
2. column heading
3. column
4. row

Page 47
1. bear
2. brood or clutch
3. mare
4. cow, calf
5. pride
6. litter
7. bevy or wedge
8. drove or flock

Page 48
1. Franklin
2. The signing of the Declaration of Independence
3. three
4. U.S. Paper Money
5. 7
6. Jackson
7. 5
8. Bill, Front Portrait, Design on Back
9. They are all U.S. symbols.
10. Answers will vary but should include a nonfiction resource.

Page 49
Answers will vary.

Page 50
1. title
2. day
3. time
4. activity
5. bus stop
6. departure time

Page 52
1.–5. Check schedule to see that activities were written in on the correct day and time.
6. water Mr. Jones's plants
7. 2 hours
8. 1 hour
9. Feed the Smiths' cats, Swim team, Dance camp
10. Tuesday
11. Monday, Wednesday, Thursday
12. A Route
13. Answers may include 2:10 P.M. or 2:40 P.M.

Page 53
Answers will vary.

Page 54
1. line graph title
2. *y*-axis
3. line
4. *x*-axis
5. bar graph title
6. scale
7. bar
8. labels

Page 56
1. 1999
2. 2007
3. 100
4. 2003
5. 9
6. grow
7. Answers will vary. *Sample answer:* The information could help people decide how many yearbooks to order next year.
8. the 4th graders' favorite subjects at Dooley Elementary
9. math
10. 15
11. language arts
12. science
13. 25
14. art, social studies
15. 100

Page 57
Graph should include the following elements:
Title: *Sample answer:* Pets from Mrs. Johnson's Class
Labels: No Pet, Dog, Cat, Fish, Other
Student questions will vary.

Page 58
1. title
2. event
3. period of time
4. date

Page 59
1. inventions
2. 1906
3. pre-sliced bread
4. 39 years
5. 60
6. between 1900 and 1910

Page 60
1. Pilgrims landed at Plymouth in Massachusetts.
2. 1775
3. 1783
4. 1789
5. The U.S. Constitution went into effect.
6. 1773
7. three months
8. Early U.S. History should be circled.
9. 1776
10. 169 years

Page 61
Time line titles will vary.
Time line should be labeled: 1945, 1955, 1960, 1965, 1970.
Check to ensure time line is correctly labeled. Check students' questions and answers for accuracy.